Wiley Global Finance is a market-leading provider of over 400 annual books, mobile applications, elearning products, workflow training tools, newsletters and websites for both professionals and consumers in institutional finance, trading, corporate accounting, exam preparation, investing, and performance management.

Maximizing Return on Investment Using ERP Applications

Nicholas

Thank you for your support for our CMU programs.

[signature]

Maximizing Return on Investment Using ERP Applications

ARTHUR J. WORSTER
THOMAS R. WEIRICH
FRANK J. C. ANDERA

WILEY

John Wiley & Sons, Inc.

Published by John Wiley & Sons, Inc., Hoboken, New Jersey.
Published simultaneously in Canada.

For general information on our other products and services or for technical support, please contact our Customer Care Department within the United States at (800) 762-2974, outside the United States at (317) 572-3993 or fax (317) 572-4002.

Wiley also publishes its books in a variety of electronic formats. Some content that appears in print may not be available in electronic books. For more information about Wiley products, visit our web site at www.wiley.com.

Library of Congress Cataloging-in-Publication Data:

Worster, Arthur J., 1944-
    Maximizing return on investment using ERP applications / Arthur J. Worster, Thomas R. Weirich, Frank J.C. Andera.
        p.   cm.
    Includes index.
    ISBN 978-1-118-42229-8 (cloth); ISBN 978-1-118-46699-5 (ebk.);
    ISBN 978-1-118-46700-8 (ebk.); ISBN 978-1-118-47612-3 (ebk.)
        1. Management information systems.   2. Business planning.   I. Weirich, Thomas R.   II. Andera, Frank J. C.   III. Title.
    HD30.213.W67   2012
    658.4'038011—dc23
                                                                    2012026255

Printed in the United States of America
10 9 8 7 6 5 4 3 2 1

For Tom Moczulski, the cofounder of our own "Dead Poet's Society," without whose courage and friendship this journey might have never started, and for my wife, children, and grandchildren, whose lives will forever be changed by the technology revolution—hopefully, in positive ways.

—Arthur J. Worster

Contents

Preface

SOME YEARS AGO, on returning from the manufacturing floor of my (coauthor Art Worster) plant, I stopped to clean my hands. There was a tub of benzene in the sink, and I dipped my hands into the solvent to get the grease off and then washed them in water. One of my colleagues came up and quickly admonished me not to do that because "Benzene is a carcinogen." My response was, "Wow, when did benzene become a carcinogen?" The fact of the matter is that it has always been, but science was just finally catching up to the relationship between chemical exposures and diseases such as cancer. What does that have to do with this book, *Maximizing Return on Investment Using ERP Applications*? The book could have been titled *Leadership and Change in an Integrated Business World*, which might have seemed to imply that our business worlds have suddenly become integrated in a sort of metaphysical change, and we are now trying to figure out how to deal with the results, but this would be wrong, similar to my experience with benzene. The business world that our enterprises exist in has always operated with integrated processes, but only over the last 15 years or so are the full effects of this integration and the techniques needed to manage integrated business processes being exposed by the introduction of integrated IT applications, such as ERP (Enterprise Resource Planning) packages. It is not a case of something new; it is a case of our knowledge of these relationships becoming known, just as in the case of benzene.

This book will lay out the case for how leadership must adapt to use this new knowledge of the world we already work in and how to develop management tools to structure our businesses to make effective use of this new knowledge. The many examples of the phenomena described in this book come from my personal experience with multiple companies and divisions of companies over the years and will serve to help the reader identify with behaviors and results that are experienced every day in most companies that are engaged in implementing or using ERP applications. First, however, let me tell you how I came to this understanding of business processes and the tools necessary to optimize business operations.

 MY OWN JOURNEY

Many years ago, I was challenged by a philosophy professor to figure out not only what I thought that I believed, but also why. His approach was to encourage us to think beyond the immediate opinions and understand the reasons from our experience or our thinking that caused us to hold those opinions. In other words, we should try to understand the relationships between the way we think and what we thought. Although not necessarily a traumatic event in my life, it did establish a pattern that led to viewing the world around me differently, that is, looking for relationships between things, rather than just understanding each individual component as an independent part, as well as working to understand the logical principles that caused these relationships to be what they are. This, in other words, was my introduction to process thinking. Without really recognizing this approach along the way as a philosophy, I found out later in my various careers that I could not seem to solve many issues or problems by simply trying to fix what appeared to be broken or dysfunctional. Issues or problems could be better understood by evaluating the relationship of the problem area with other areas that either affected or were affected by what I was trying to fix.

This process-focused approach to the world that I lived in eventually became a natural part of everything that I did, and when integrated ERP applications came along in the 1990s (this is the time that they first became practical for most businesses), it was natural for me to look to the relationships between the various functions that were supported, rather than just trying to resolve issues within a single function. That is really what this book is about— adopting a process-focused approach to understanding business functions and the IT applications that support them and to propose a program to govern the process of using these systems to manage a permanent continuous business improvement program based on rapidly expanding capabilities. I think that the story of how I came to adopt the "Leadership and Change" model that is presented in this book is useful to explain how and why this is important in providing the opportunity to make a step-function (transformational, rather than incremental) change to business results.

My early years were spent designing, building, and operating chemical processes, plants, and divisions, where engineering relationships were based on science. This experience was invaluable in building process-thinking disciplines that have served me well in the second half of my career. However, my journey to a leadership model that incorporated these principles started for real in 1989. The path that I took during the last two decades is a good illustration of the problem that we face today—that of trying to develop leaders with the ability to effectively and easily (relatively speaking) use IT business applications to optimize business processes and, in doing so, deliver improved business results. We all know many of the catchy phrases and adages about how this works:

> "All business processes have been perfectly designed to produce today's business results." (Paraphrased from many authors)

> "The definition of insanity is doing the same thing over and over and expecting different results." (Attributed to many, including Albert Einstein and Benjamin Franklin)

In addition, virtually every business I have encountered during the last two decades has invested in a significant number of improvement programs, all of which promised to deliver improved business results, if only . . . ! This could, I suppose, be the result of either awful leaders or a lack of knowledge of how to arrange and manage businesses for positive results. However, my experience has told me that this is not a credible explanation in the vast majority of cases. More to the point, this assessment of leadership doesn't lead to knowledge of the failure mechanisms or how to manage change processes to produce intended results in an integrated business world. Rather, we believe that good leaders simply don't have the right tools or understanding to deal with the magnitude of change that using these applications provides or how to ensure that they achieve the returns that are inherently possible by using them.

Because my experiences are similar to those of others, I think that my journey will resonate with many readers. In this book, I join with my two coauthors to share what we have found out during this period regarding how to effectively use IT business applications to produce continuous improvement in business operations and ultimately in business results. In telling this story, we refer to most of the programs that have come and gone (or come and stayed) during this period and explain what we learned from them and how we have incorporated them into a leadership approach that is focused on producing tangible business results. We tell the story in chronological order, even though at times it hardly seemed to move from one experience to the next. The discussion focuses on a frustration that was felt more than two decades ago when I was part of a division turn-around team tasked with rescuing a business that had fallen on hard times. In short order, one went or was dragged through many "programs" that were formulated to promote a concept that was usually valid and often even insightful. The frustration, however, came from the practice of developing a formulated approach in order to solve one conceptual problem we had discovered. What we realized was that all of the problems were part of a larger system issue and that often the actual source of the failures was in the interactions among various functions or processes, or the reactions of one part of the process in response to the actions of another part. In other words, the entire problem we observed had to be considered as part of a larger process, and just as in designing chemical process units, the solution had to involve all of the working components of the system. It often seemed that what we worked on one day were unintended consequences of other actions taken on other parts of the system earlier.

The Early Years (1963–1973)

There were significant changes happening in the ways businesses were organized and managed and the tools available to identify, analyze, plan, and execute changes. At that point in history, a number of disciplines were finally coming together, with the logical relationship between them being better understood. This ultimately resulted from the development of business applications technology. It was becoming possible to develop software that could integrate the effects of transactions (events that the company performed and recorded as part of doing business), and it could be applied simultaneously across different functions within the business in real time. Although this seems like an obvious advantage, the issue was that our businesses were generally not organized such that the implementation of these systems would be easy. The business relationships between functions were not fully understood as a continuous process, and in many cases, these logical inconsistencies were embedded in arcane methods of operating and reporting on the business. All of these were supported by objectives, improvement programs, and other cultural and political barriers to making smooth transactions. I am getting ahead of myself, though. Looking back, my first experience with any kind of transactional integration was nearly 50 years ago when I learned how to perform what I now know as MRP I (Material Requirements Planning) manually using VISIrecords from tub files (open tubs that housed large ledger cards on which records were kept of inventory and usages of parts and assemblies) to perform parts ordering based on manufacturing requirements. My recollection is that we didn't even call it that at the time, although time may have dimmed my memory. In any event, we now had Bills of Materials, restocking orders, parts lists, and more that we could use to ensure that the materials were available when needed, and that there was less need for excess inventory because the time-phased demand was better known and better used. Today, this seems like a simple thing, but in 1963, it brought tangible benefits to the production operations. It was also the first time that I realized that what I was learning were the logical relationships between real-world functions that could be used to transform the way even a small department operated.

Foundations (1973–1988)

Before becoming involved in business operations, I spent nearly 20 years designing, building, and operating specialty chemical plants and divisions. During these years, IT was for the most part a set of tractor-paper reports (so named for the early printer's drive mechanisms that required perforated edges so that the drive wheel could grip the paper) that were collated and run at division headquarters and delivered to the plant early the following week. Most of my time was spent learning a process approach to both operations and problem solving. In this case, it had to do with chemical process or material-flow process in order to increase the capacity, efficiency, and output from the plants that I had responsibility for. As any good chemical process engineer well knows, the ability to understand a chemical process is a combination of knowledge of the science being employed, and, more important, the ability to see and understand the relationship between components, sequences, reactions, and so on. This was not the case with business departments. Without the availability of "integrated" business systems, individuals in each function began to design work processes within their functional areas. Discussions then ensued between these functions on how to relate them to one another and, more often than not, resulted in disagreements that the strongest manager tended to win. This was often to the detriment of the business, but since the processes were not understood, nobody knew.

As an example, one would guess at how much our production would be for a given period, factor it for yield, calculate the need for each material, and tell procurement what to order. Procurement then would negotiate supply and price with suppliers. The problem, of course, is that this is a pretty simple example that worked acceptably for some plants, but more complex examples became anywhere from unpredictable to disastrous. Nevertheless, successful management of the physical operation of the plant was directly dependent on the ability to understand individual pieces, figure out what the relationship was between the pieces, design a means to manage the correct handoff of information from one to the other, and then coordinate them as an orchestra conductor would. At the time, I can remember having multiple units in each of three vertically integrated departments and having the flexibility to move production from one department to any of the three in the next stage. The trick was arranging them in an order such that we were able to push the maximum amount of production through the combined departments—logical relationships. We used these manual processes to predict human resource requirements, raw material requirements, capital improvements, and so on. Usually, this was done by ensuring that any errors would be on the side of having too much and never running out of whatever was predicted. Our business had a large margin on sales, and we could get away with inefficiencies. Yet we had no automated way to define the relationships and manage the processes in real time. Accessible IT in the form of personal computers was still 10 years away and it was closer to 15 years before personal computers became practical for large numbers of people and locations.

Manufacturing Operations Optimization (1989–1991)

In 1989, I was asked to be part of a team with the objective of figuring out what was happening in a business that had appeared profitable, was quickly losing profitability, and was either going to be set back on a successful path or shut down. The business had grown over many years, with product lines being expanded and diminished, but with each one being operated like a separate business. Finding synergies between departments was possible, and the operating strategies and support departments allowed for combining several similar functions into business-wide support departments—such as plant maintenance, quality assurance, distribution, and others. This was also the time that MRP II (Manufacturing Resources Planning) was being implemented at the plant, requiring a broader, more integrated view of operations. The relationship between sales planning, sales forecasting, manufacturing capacity calculation and timing planning, warehousing, and distribution was becoming more obvious. However, the IT applications continued to be entirely within functions and often within functions inside of functional departments. Our version of MRP II at the time was basically a tracking system that would manage shop floor work through a series of work stations, and the product would be tracked through them. There was no real understanding of the relationship between the pieces. Sales did forecasting, manufacturing defined manufacturing capacity and production streams, procurement worked to ensure that the production floor never ran out of raw materials, and so on. MRP II first drew attention to things such as the definition of manufacturing capacity based on line speeds (a technical design element that was set for each product), constraint points, and line availability. Although the concept of MRP II is a closed-loop planning process encompassing logistics flows within the operation, early systems struggled to provide full integration between functions.

In our case, integration was achieved with the help of spreadsheets that could align functions such as finished goods reordering to manufacturing capacity and provide input to production planning. Because many of the pieces did not easily communicate with one another, it also provided both the opportunity and the challenge to figure out what data needed to flow between functions, what form it needed to be in, and how changes in the output of one system influenced the operation of the next. A lot of time was spent in late-night design meetings trying to figure out how to make this happen. Each system was based on different data models and fed into or out of different processes. Ultimately, we discovered that we could factor demand from the finished goods systems in days for each of 8,800 end-items to create demand that could then be converted to a production campaign that fit onto the production equipment, repeating manufacturing cycles every three weeks. This factor was combined with the days in the production cycle and the time from production for goods to reach the warehouse to create a master production schedule that could be ramped up or down to accommodate plant shutdowns and other interruptions. How this was done is really not the important point here—the key point is that we were able to understand how each of the parts logically related to the others and could create a system to keep them in balance. It is this knowledge of the logic of relationships that is the key to understanding how full business-wide ERP suites have to be designed across business processes. I think that it is also useful to point out here that recognizing these relationships, defining them, and quantifying how they work with one another is more obvious in smaller, but not necessarily less complex, processes. We tend to get lost in size when confronted with massive organizations and operating units. The fact is, however, that segmenting the units into more discrete operational pieces to analyze them can lead to the same discoveries and then can roll the discovered relationships into comprehensive understanding. This understanding is there just waiting to be found.

Business Support Optimization (1991–1994)

By 1991, it had become obvious that the division was in serious difficulty. First, a study in market segmentation drew a picture of a market that had maintained the illusion of a specialty product for decades and had discovered that the products used were really commodities, resulting in a collapse of the price the market would pay. Second, a study of competitive manufacturing costs indicated that among the eight suppliers, this company had the next to the highest manufacturing cost, which in a commodity business predicts failure. The results of this study caused us to look more deeply into the high manufacturing costs. Some examples of what we found were the following issues.

In general, the sales department would predict what its sales would be for all seven different sales/distribution centers, each of which would place orders on manufacturing. The sales forecasts were built around actual shipments to a few major customers, but primarily to distributors around North America. Sales numbers indicated the level of sales, and the volume of manufacturing was roughly equivalent to the sales volumes, but mysteriously, the total inventory dollars continued to rise and nobody had an explanation. Beyond that, it seemed that the larger it got, the higher the number of back orders also became. Although there were some common systems (particularly, in the distribution centers), they were not used the same and might as well have been different systems at times. The problems and numbers just kept getting worse, and the departments dug in to construct cases to prove that other groups were responsible—blame was the name of the game because the systems simply could not provide answers. Ultimately, the issue was resolved when the sales administration department that calculated sales by salesperson for compensation incentive purposes was moved to the business support group, where we discovered that sales incentives were based on gross sales and that same number was being reported as sales for forecasting production needs. In fact, at the end of each month, excess "sales" would be sent to distributors to achieve sales targets and then would often be shipped back at the start of the next month. Resolution required acknowledgment of these practices (which were not known to the division staff) and adjustment of compensation programs so that net sales would be used both for sales targets and forecasting. Beyond that, the system to relate finished goods inventory levels by product to production campaign schedules, described previously, was completed, and actual inventory levels were used to order new products, rather than gross sales numbers. Resolution became possible when the logic between components became known and quantified. Later in this book, as we discuss ERP programs, this principle will become one of the key drivers of both business process improvements and cultural and political resistance at all levels.

While evaluating production capacity and utilization of the manufacturing lines, we also encountered issues. We knew what the design line speed was for the production of each product (which was pretty well set). However, we did not know what the utilization time was for the availability of equipment (percentage of 168 hours a week that the machine would operate at design speeds). It turned out that each department had a different formula for reporting utilization, which resulted in several different estimations of capacity. Maintenance reported availability as 168 hours (hours in a calendar week) minus unscheduled line stoppages, but manufacturing reported actual hours that the machinery operated, with little tracking of stoppage time. It turns out that the line would stop even for quality assurance checks. This happened often when the QA technician would be on break, for scheduled or unscheduled maintenance, as well as for line changeovers that tradition held required two shifts. As it turned out, it was actually comfortably fewer than eight hours when the activities were sequenced and done one after the other, rather than based on a timed schedule that was years old. Without agreed-on formulas, definitions of downtime, scheduling parameters, and so on, it was virtually impossible to develop programs to address the issues. We developed and implemented spreadsheets to define and track each based on a single version of the truth, with great resistance from each department that had used its own version to elevate its departmental objectives. Imagine how this plays out in an ERP world where the integration of the system requires that there be a single design. If the basic differences between perceived departmental needs are not understood, they are virtually impossible to resolve. It is the understanding of these relationships that is the key.

The main point here is that without some integration of the process needs, operating parameters of the various departments, and alignment of approaches, issues became political battles mostly focused on blame, rather than on problem resolution. This is typically not because of bad people; however, the disastrous effect that it has on the performance of the business can be dramatic. For this reason, knowing these relationships provides a key to working through the issues described later in this book.

In order to get resolution of these issues, we combined all of the departments that were affected by these internal integration points (not that we knew to call them that at the time), moving them from their traditional homes in sales, manufacturing, controller, and logistics and putting them all under one leadership with sufficient IT support to redesign the business processes, design the functional changes that were necessary to the legacy IT applications, and implement the now "integrated" changes to the programs that supported all of the areas affected. This approach is hardly one that can be used in most circumstances, and consequently, over the years, we have developed an approach that takes issues such as this and provides a means to deal with these interdepartmental design challenges at the executive levels, which can then be implemented through all of the operational departments. You can start to see how solving these issues manually and early on helps develop the ability to see businesses as a collection of business processes and, furthermore, how these business processes produce the results that you experience today. The examples (described here) are the problems that had prevented a small business ($130M/yr revenue) from resolving its issues and ones that nearly caused the business to close. If you multiply these issues and add the complexity that exists in very large organizations, you can see the need for new ways of looking at business performance to identify the unintended consequences of past actions that may have addressed immediate needs but brought unwanted side effects.

 ## BUSINESS PROCESS REENGINEERING AND SAP

Based on the success we had experienced in the business just described, I moved to a larger role, working with many divisions of the business group that all operated on a collection of different legacy applications, most of which were also losing money. In this case, my challenge was finding a way to identify the causes of the failures, as we did in the first business, and to design changes to business processes that could be incorporated into massive rewrites of the legacy applications' layers that supported them. It just happened that one of the businesses was in the middle of an implementation of an "integrated" solution to its business problems (ERP). In preparing the business group to move from the legacy systems and adopt an ERP platform for their IT applications (SAP), I had the opportunity to take 75 days of specific courses that covered the capability of every functional area in the company. The experience I gained in directing the rewrite of the business applications in the previous business had provided me with the knowledge that allowed me to understand the relationships, touch points, and interdependencies of the various functional configurations. Most of my months of training consisted of developing an understanding of how cross-functional business processes worked in the ERP system, which enabled me to take a process-focused look at the other design work we were doing. The history of my career is not the important thing to take away from this book. It is, rather, the series of learning points and the insight that I acquired over all of these decades to be able to look across functions of organizations and, through observation, see not only where issues existed by discovering the evidence, but also use the logical relationship between functions to know where to go to resolve base issues. We will describe later in this book why it is problematic for most organizations today to develop this thought process and the skills required, due to the cultural and political boundaries that have developed over the years, but it will also become obvious that the inability to do this can permanently handicap an organization and must be addressed by a new form of operational governance.

The purpose of introducing you to these ideas is to point out that the path to fully understand how cross-functional business processes can make or break an organization and how IT business applications are used to evaluate, define, implement, and institutionalize new processes is a difficult one. It was pointed out in 1991 by Peter G. W. Keen that

> Senior business executives lack a well-established management process for taking charge of IT. . . . Business managers consequently have not developed the kind of experience and expertise in IT that they have in finance, human resources, and accounting.[1]

This remains true today, and we are just starting to develop educational programs that address this need. If you look at undergraduate degree programs, most universities have a clear separation between IT programs and business programs. Many business degree programs offer some requirements and elective options for students to take business information systems courses, but these for the most part teach material on the technology itself and offer little insight into how these integrated applications actually determine business results. Some universities have integrated programs; however, these are not prevalent, and professors often don't spend the time to teach a comprehensive view of how the two interact. IT professors tend to teach IT and how to deploy it to support a business. Business professors tend to teach their functional specialties, such as accounting, finance, purchasing and supply management, operations management, logistics management, and others but rarely teach how integrated applications logic is used to create sustainable business processes. Prior to the introduction of ERP applications, this was a practical approach to including these courses in our curriculum. It is left to each student to piece these together when he or she graduates and enters business. Nearly always, however, new graduates will be hired into a single function where they will learn how to apply their academic preparation to organize, supervise, manage, and ultimately lead that function. M.B.A. programs tend to follow the same pattern, resulting in the vast majority of leaders in business having been educated and socialized into a functionally restrictive silo environment, where learning cross-functional relationships can lead to political issues around "turf."

 ## THIS BOOK

This book is meant to deal with that situation as we find it, provide analysis of how this adversely affects business performance, suggest a method to approach working within the process to help resolve issues at all levels, and improve business performance and Return on Investment in IT business applications, particularly ERP programs. Most of today's commentary on business transformation using ERP programs focuses either on a traditional set of project management skills and programs or the commentary focuses on yet more technology that is going to supersede everything we currently have and create a whole new, perfectly tuned and operating business world. This focus on either project techniques or instant technological solutions has resulted in what we have today—many well-delivered programs using all of the technology tools and management techniques available. Often they are successful in completing the scope of the projects on time, on budget, using effective technology. However, the vast majority of them are still considered unsuccessful, at least because of their failure to deliver the business benefits that the Return on Investment case was built on.

How can this be? In our opinion, it is most certainly not the technology, which continues to provide exciting opportunities, or the management techniques, which are well understood. If it is not these two aspects, it is our contention that the failures lies within the business itself and how the organization deals with the concepts it uses to understand the relationship between the business and the transformation programs. We show how leading and changing businesses in an integrated world requires deeper understanding of the characteristics of all organizations, which either enables us to maximize or prevents us from maximizing the Return on Investment from ERP programs.

In Part I of this book, we look at different approaches to how leadership should view the organization as an integrated enterprise and what this change in perception might suggest.

In Part II, we look specifically at five aspects of running a business and suggest how a different approach to looking at each of them may provide new insight.

Finally, in Part III, we propose a program governance model that can help guide an organization through the transformation in business leadership that will produce tangible business benefits.

As an added topic, in Chapter 12, we briefly address what the future might hold for companies that are successful in getting their houses in order so that they can take full advantage of all of the ERP capability that is available today and that we can see coming in the future.

It is our honor and privilege to share this information with current and future executives as you fine-tune your leadership approaches for using ERP applications as tools that deliver business performance.

We hope you enjoy reading this book!

—Arthur J. Worster

 NOTE

1. Peter G. W. Keen, *Shaping the Future* (Cambridge: Harvard Business School Press, 1991).

Acknowledgements

THERE HAVE BEEN MANY OVER THE YEARS who contributed to the knowledge and experience that are reflected here and from whom many lessons were learned. Process thinking was first introduced to me by my chemical process engineer colleagues—Tom Scacco, Doug Brown, and others. For the confidence that a small plant production manager could design and oversee new plants, thanks to Frank Fackler for his support and encouragement.

For providing the leadership models that at once inspired me and ultimately guided my own learning and development, thanks to U.S. Air Force general George B. Simler and John Lauer, who modeled the energy, vision, and commitment to accomplish the mission. Later, for teaching the importance of values-based leadership, I thank our own "Dead Poet's Society" and the learning environment that we created—thanks, in particular, to Tom Moczulski, Pat Gray, Alison Smith, Steve O'Donnell, and Ed Soriano, without whose honesty and openness we could not have been successful. For providing me with insight into business process management, thanks to John Civerolo, Dr. E. Earl Burch, and Andrew Spanyi, through whose support the interrelationships among the five business aspects described here were first illuminated, analyzed, and ultimately understood.

To the business leaders who entrusted me with their businesses' futures, learning how ERP applications worked to define, institutionalize, and manage their business processes, from David Shavzin, Dave McDaniel, and Robert Hawkins to the entire Dial Executive Team led by Bernie Welle, Rad Conrad, and Evon Jones. To Mark Bilger, Dan Allison, and their leadership teams for the opportunity to work to build an organization based on providing business value to global clients, through the development of which we learned many lessons that are expressed in this book.

Finally, to my colleagues at Central Michigan University who had the vision to develop an M.B.A. curriculum based on using ERP applications to teach business fundamentals and for accepting me as a business adviser to that program. Particular thanks to Dean Mike Fields, for the initial vision to expand the well-developed undergraduate SAP programs into an M.B.A. Graduate Concentration and Certificate; to Dean Dan Vetter, for his unwavering support for the programs and their value both to graduate education and to the business community; and to Dean Chuck Crespy, for his continuing support to solidify the program that ultimately led to this book.

Finally, thanks to my two coauthors, without whose support this project would have never left the gate.

—Arthur J. Worster

▪ ▪ ▪

I thank my wife, Sharon, and our five daughters, who have encouraged and supported me in my teaching and research endeavors.

—Thomas R. Weirich

▪ ▪ ▪

I extend a special thank-you to Mary Jo, my wife and closest friend, for her support and encouragement.

—Frank J. C. Andera

Introduction

MANY BOOKS have been written about each of the topics discussed in this book, and many of them contain well-formulated approaches to dealing with one aspect of business or another. Many of these books, ideas, programs, and/or approaches will be referenced in this book and supported in the discussions, while many more that are not mentioned are very likely equally useful in certain circumstances. This book takes the view that although much has been created during the last two decades to help organizations use integrated business applications effectively, failures defined as not achieving intended Return on Investment from ERP investment have continued to dominate our experience. The book is not a memoir, although it is based on very specific examples we have experienced over the years. It is not written as a purely academic exploration, either, although it does postulate new thinking. It is written experientially, meaning that it is based on designed approaches, observation of the factors that led to success or failure, rethinking of project and program designs, more observation, and finally a decision that failures were not so much the result of improperly observing but of framing our observations through the wrong lenses.

This book starts with these assumptions:

- Basic project management knowledge and toolsets are available and used by skilled practitioners. The proliferation of PMP (Project Management Professional) certified practitioners and the development of implementation toolsets thoroughly integrated into the ERP products themselves have been extensive during the last decade or so.
- Expertly skilled consultants are available and have been hired to design and implement the technical aspects of the program. While it is certainly still possible to select poorly from the large consulting pools available, there is virtually no functional area where you cannot find true experts in their functions.

1

- An expert business project team can be assembled that has sufficient knowledge of both the current business process and the proposed changes to support the program. This doesn't say that the business has necessarily done this, but the knowledge is available, more often than not.
- Executive leadership of the business understands the project and the requirements to get the program executed properly. There is nearly always an Executive Steering Committee (ESC) assembled, with at least nominal oversight of the program.

In other words, the starting point looks very much like most projects that have been conducted during the last few years. Most of them have been successful in getting the applications implemented (although often late and over budget) and the organization is operating on and becoming accustomed to the new functionality.

The problem, however, is that either the project was not based on clear financial improvement objectives (Return on Investment) or else the planned results have not materialized, despite all of the previous assumptions being adhered to faithfully. It is our assumption that this can be viewed as either good news or bad news, as the story goes. The bad news, of course, is that you have spent a lot of money and resources on implementing the ERP applications and have failed to achieve the Return on Investment on which the program was justified. The good news, however, is that in the vast majority of cases, the benefits originally envisioned are still there and available if the business takes the time to evaluate why they were not achieved and figures out how to make the necessary changes to achieve them now. We will describe in Chapter 4 a new way of viewing Return on Investment that includes the concept that potential returns exist independent of the project you have undertaken and that there is an optimal design of the business that will allow for improved business performance.

This book evaluates this common phenomenon and provides a new way of looking at ERP-driven business-improvement programs in general. It calls for a new way of looking at several key business fundamentals, essentially a paradigm shift, to use a phrase in common usage a decade ago, or, as we will refer to it, a contextual shift in how you perceive these basic aspects of your business. There have been many models for learning over the years; however, the one that we will use here is adopted from Dr. James Milojkovic and his work in cognitive psychology. This, as well as the others that may have meaning for the individual reader, basically dissects the way we think and learn into layers.

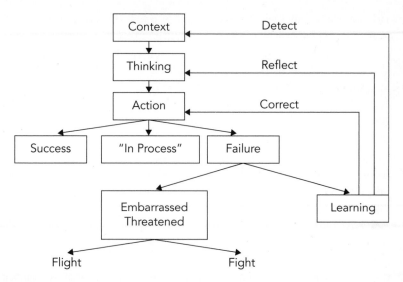

EXHIBIT I.1 Triple Loop Learning Model
Source: © 1993, 2012, Dr. James Milojkovic, Knowledge Passion, Inc. Reproduced with permission.

The purpose is to differentiate these layers so that we can develop ways to "learn" for each of them. This is particularly poignant when we are trying to understand better why smart, well-educated leadership teams with a portfolio full of tools to manage ERP programs continue to leave so much on the table. Exhibit I.1 presents Dr. Milojkovic's Triple Loop Learning Model.

To define that more clearly, we need to think about our learning process—not classroom learning (although that also applies here), but the way we learn how to evaluate what we see or calculate in the world around us, because the way we view the world we are presented with will ultimately determine how we perceive that it operates. Simple examples of this abound. Take, for example, the case of several people observing an act and, depending on race, economic class, upbringing, nationality, and many other factors, will have completely different ideas of what they have observed. There is only one factual version of what happened, and yet, based on our predispositions, we may see many different things. The same is often true of how we view our business and evaluate both its organization and its performance. We discuss how this Triple Loop Learning Model applies to how we perceive our business as it relates to achieving our business goals using ERP applications in this

Introduction. Later, in Part II, we specifically apply this concept to five different aspects of business that affect our ability to produce intended results.

First, however, let's discuss this model and then come back to each level and discuss examples of how this applies to ERP Return on Investment opportunities:

- We call the first level "action," and it is how we learn simple skills. Either we are taught or we learn through trial and error, but, ultimately, we learn what to do and what not to do. That's why we don't touch a hot stove. If we perform the action correctly, we are rewarded with success. If not, then we discover that we have made an error, resulting in failure. This provides us with the opportunity to learn from our experience, figure out what to do to correct our failure, and take the action again. We can repeat this step as many times as it takes, as we continue to learn why our actions failed. The alternative is that we react in fear and fail to take the opportunity to learn, but, for our purposes here, we will assume that there is a commitment to learning and continuous improvement, both as an individual and as an organization.
- We call the second level "thinking," meaning that we learn how the things we see are connected, and we learn the effects of these connections as a result of actions that we take. If we present certain materials to a prospective client, we get the sale. This level of learning takes place in a number of ways, because it typically takes more understanding to figure out how to react to failures. The ways in which we reflect on our failures (or our projected failures, in many cases) may include more formal learning (M.B.A. program), conferring with colleagues (staff discussions), mentoring (formal or informal), hiring employees with new skills and/or experience to broaden our thought processes, or using consultants to gain access to their experience. In all of these cases, the task is to gain access to knowledge of how the failure occurred, what the probable causes are, and what the possible solutions might be and then to construct another approach that could result in success. Ultimately, we try it again, and if we still don't succeed, we follow the same routine again until we eventually do succeed. Organizations spend much of their leadership time and resources to ensure that resources are available with sufficient knowledge to design successful approaches in the first place or to resolve issues as they occur.
- We call the third level "context," meaning that it defines how we interpret the things we see. We have found over the years that for many leaders,

recognition of the need to drive this kind of change is difficult to envision or to manage. Both from a personal and a business standpoint, however, understanding this level of change can be the key to unlock success in many areas, not the least of which is designing, implementing, and managing in an integrated business world. As an example, Return on Investment, defined as cost savings or revenue enhancements, exists in business whether we are able to recognize or recover it. The common way is to fix a problem and, in doing so, achieve some benefits that either have or haven't been quantified beforehand. The thought process that Return on Investment exists and can be recognized, independent of a project, causes us to take a whole different view of what might be possible. This is the subject of Chapter 4.

Now, let's take a closer look at the Triple Loop Learning Model and use examples as the model pertains to ERP applications of (1) action, (2) thinking, and (3) context.

ACTION

We are sure that there are many examples of applying this type of learning on ERP projects. Very simply, once a functional design team, either by itself or in cross-functional groups, decides on how it would like a business process component to work (perhaps a transaction, for example), the configurator will set the configuration tables and then run the transaction so that the team can see the results. This step will be repeated in an iterative process until the group agrees that the design goals have been met. As an example, let's use a raw material receipt against a purchase order. In this case, the design team wants to ensure that the quantities of goods are received into the inventory location and in the inventory type that is in the design (maybe an intermediate inventory location in a quality assurance hold status) and will also want to ensure that the purchase order is updated properly, that the tolerance limits have been met, that the general ledger cost element has been properly posted, that the accounts payable file has been updated, and more. The corrective actions may be simple or may require the team to talk through the results of the configuration, but the bottom line is that the task can be repeated without damage until the correct results are achieved. This level of learning is repeated throughout the project, right up to and including the way that end-user training is conducted prior to going live with the new functionality.

 **THINKING**

This level of learning is the primary one that organizations use to lead, change, and manage their organizations during their existence. A typical monthly staff meeting includes a review of past period performance and identification of those areas where the results were different from expectations, hopefully, on both the upside and the downside. In the case of the downside, the discussion centers around the reasons for the organization's failure to produce the expected or predicted results. In healthy staff organizations, this discussion will include all of the various aspects of the business and the differing perspectives of the staff managers to reflect on the results, propose possible explanations, create possible solutions, and agree on action steps to change the results for the next meeting. As a simple example to conceptualize, let's use total inventory. If the inventory is higher than the predicted levels, it could be because sales were less than anticipated, either because of some market shift or because of poor forecasting (or other reasons, but this is a simple example). It could also be because production produced more than had been anticipated for any number of reasons. Perhaps the company decided that it would need to take some downtime and it was building inventory prior to that occasion. It could be production planning, which might have simply made an error or needed to extend a particular production material for scheduling purposes. It could be a quality assurance issue, where materials were being held for evaluation, and, therefore, additional materials had to be made to ship. There are many more examples for any specific business.

This same level of thinking is represented in design meetings where the issues with the current business performance are discussed, new approaches proposed and tested, and then configurations completed to see if they produce improved business results. This is the primary thought process that businesses use to plan, operate, analyze, and correct their current and future business performance.

 **CONTEXT**

This is the learning level that this book primarily deals with. If you take the assumptions at the start of this Introduction that many of the key fundamentals of designing and implementing ERP applications have been strengthened over the years and these systems have been viable for the majority of businesses, you then have to think beyond what has not worked up to now. There is a reason that many publications, from professional journals to airline magazines, have published articles that emphasize over and over again the need to design programs, including all of the components that have now been there for years. Yet even though a majority of individual projects are actually completed today (an improvement over a decade ago) and get closer and closer to being on time and on budget, we continue to bemoan the lack of tangible business results to justify continued investments. If we are not to simply repeat our past experience, there must be something else that is standing in the way of our achieving improved performance using these applications.

We believe that these failures can be attributed to the way in which we think about several aspects of the business, or the context of our thinking process. In our personal lives, our opinions on social issues are very likely shaped by our religious beliefs, which are the context with which we view them. In politics, our view of whether any one bill or agency is right or wrong is very likely informed by our belief in the role of government. There is nothing wrong with this; it is the way we, as human beings, think. We all have contexts, cognitive principles, paradigms, or whatever you would like to call them that help us frame what we see into an order that allows us to create understanding at the "thinking" level. This is also true about more mundane areas of our lives than the spiritual or the political, and these contextual prisms through which we view our business world shade our analysis of how to address what are, after all, extremely intransigent issues.

The case we present is that we know how to design actions, we know how to think about design issues, but taking a different view of how some business fundamentals work on a contextual level can provide insights into how to reverse our past experience and achieve the benefits that we need to address the challenges we all face with processes, competitors, customers, vendors, and the myriad of other issues that come our way.

PART ONE

A Leadership Perspective

PART I DEALS with defining the issues of Enterprise Resource Planning (ERP) programs and how these programs create the need for a new perspective for leadership to address the problems of achieving the business benefits required to compete in today's economic climate. It provides the reader with a thorough discussion of how leadership principles both define the path forward and put into place structures to help executives conceptualize and resolve cultural and political conflicts.

This section concludes with an evaluation and an assessment of the evolution of ERP programs and how this evolution has affected the ability of today's leaders to keep up with the potential of new integrated systems that are being implemented in today's enterprises.

- Chapter 1, "The Law of Unintended Consequences": This chapter specifically focuses on the phenomenon of unintended consequences and its impact on enterprises.

- Chapter 2, "Leadership and Change in an Integrated Business World": This chapter presents the issue of how leaders struggle to adapt to changes caused by the implementation of ERP applications.
- Chapter 3, "A Historical Business Perspective of ERP": This chapter provides an overview of the historical events of the ERP environment discussed throughout the text.

CHAPTER ONE

The Law of Unintended Consequences

"Long-term commitment to new learning and new philosophy is required of any management that seeks transformation. The timid and the faint-hearted, and people that expect quick results, are doomed to disappointment."

—*W. Edwards Deming*, Out of the Crisis

 INTRODUCTION

Going far back into history, philosophers have commented on the phenomenon of unintended consequences, both for good and for bad. Various references go back to Locke or Burke as talking about this principle in general terms, and it was a primary element of Adam Smith's "invisible hand" as one of the guiding principles of modern economics, albeit in Smith's case the unintended consequences were the positive effects of the "invisible hand." For the purpose of this book, we refer to this law as a primary reason that well-intentioned actions taken in a functionally organized world create unforeseen negative consequences across

11

an enterprise and define how the conversion to ERP programs contributes to the illumination of the logical relationships that cause these to occur. With this illumination comes the opportunity to design and implement changes within an organization that will more closely produce intended results.[1]

 ## WHAT IS THE LAW OF UNINTENDED CONSEQUENCES?

Everyone has heard the expression "It is what it is." Although obviously tautological (inherently true), the statement still begs a couple of questions:

- Exactly what is it and is what we perceive it to be what it actually is?
- If we really understand what it is, wouldn't it be nice to know how it got this way so that we could figure out how to either change the current state or use it more effectively?

We are not suggesting that large efforts be expended to rehash history or agonize over past decisions, which may be perceived as errors, in hindsight. Instead, a few examples follow of how business approaches evolve over time into situations that were never intended and that present significant obstacles to improvement. Furthermore, regardless of whether the intent is to drive improvements (our view is that it always should), changes necessitated by the explosion of IT business applications technology are unavoidable as we adopt an integrated view of business. This is the product of integrated systems exposing the logical relationships between functions that were not fully understood or supported in the past. Far from criticizing past organizational development, we believe that these approaches evolved as natural constructs developed to model past practices and understanding. All that being said, however, in order to effectively use current Enterprise Resource Planning (ERP) platforms to improve business results, business leaders must make organizational changes from functional alignment to truly integrated business processes.

Let's start with integrated business systems themselves. The integrated business applications platform in an enterprise has several roles, including

1. Execute transactions.
2. Record and store transaction records.
3. Provide "real-time" view.
4. Manage designed business processes.

5. Establish internal controls.
6. Provide an analysis of business performance.

Furthermore, the integrated business applications platform

1. Provides a way to execute and record transactions. In this regard, it is different only in presentation and organization from traditional systems of the past.
2. Offers a means to record and store the results of transactions over time, for the purpose of organizing, collating, and reporting on them.
3. Allows a "real-time" view of the physical and financial condition of the enterprise. (This is almost always true of business components such as sales orders to date, inventory levels, and so on. It is somewhat less true at a higher level, where functions such as consolidations and reconciliation accounts are not processed in real time.)
4. Manages business processes that have been designed to both meet commercial needs of the business and produce optimal business results (regardless of whether this has been done correctly). This is a key point because a business process, in our terms, is cross-functional and must be designed and implemented across all of the affected functions. Whatever the business process design is, however, the ERP platform will institutionalize them for good or for bad.
5. Builds a design into an integrated system that provides internal controls (segregation of responsibilities) and controls over processes that can be audited to ensure compliance with regulations (such as governance, risk, compliance, and functionality—GRC in SAP and other ERP platforms have other tools to do this). Beyond these controls, however, it is possible to design processes that serve as cross-verification of internal relationships between business departments that can provide insight into problems, errors, inefficiencies, instabilities, and other risk-associated factors that arise in every corporation. While insight into how this could be achieved can be learned through the audit tools, real comprehension of how these integration points work is necessary to create the tools that are needed.

To illustrate this point, let's look at a couple of examples of management systems that have grown over time to become problems that are difficult to resolve, even though they grew through well-intended actions taken without sufficient knowledge of logical relationships within the business and have resulted in serious unintended consequences.

MANAGEMENT SYSTEMS

The first example is based on experience with a number of companies and draws on historical events that happened, but not all with one company. The example also has elements that are consistent with the results but are constructed to explain observations. They may have occurred as part of the story but could just as well have been the result of other equally problematic actions or policies. When we are trying to explain situations and how they came to exist, it is useful to understand the organizations as they existed when the current situation was evolving. This requires taking a process view of how the designs developed over time and usually under multiple leaders. This example, however, draws on real experiences and points out the value an integrated system can bring to enterprise risk management functions. It also, by pointing out why situations come into existence, provides insight into the challenges in taking them apart. Ultimately, it points to the reasons outstanding executives find themselves trapped in the cultural and political processes meant to serve them and without all of the tools to resolve the issues that entrap them, as we will discuss in Chapter 6. The political process in executive groups that renders this so difficult was well covered by Chris Argyris in his book *Overcoming Organizational Defenses*, in which he points out the reasons that highly effective executives fail to collectively resolve difficult issues.[2] While true, the increase in knowledge of logical business relationships and a better understanding of the inevitable consequences of actions can help make issues more factual and less political.

Example 1: Services Industry

The first example is in the services industry. The purpose is to demonstrate how certain organizational structures, procedures, and processes that are dysfunctional today came into existence through perfectly proper, if not thoroughly thought-out, actions. Even though the illustration is a collection of events from different companies, it is representative of processes that exist in any number of companies and industries. This example helps answer the questions of

1. How do these organizations develop over time?
2. Why aren't these issues obvious during the years as they are evolving?
3. How can these issues be detected earlier?
4. What are the types of organizational support elements that have to be in place in order to work through the conflicts and agree on resolution,

recognizing that over time the natural evolution of the structures comes with significant cultural, political, and potentially even legal issues?

The Start of the Story

Services Industry Corporation (SIC) incorporated decades ago as a privately held company focusing on a number of major accounts where it provided information technology (IT)—related services. The breadth of services at the outset included hardware, data centers, and software support (either development, maintenance, or both). The business grew dramatically at the initial accounts, with each account operating as if it were a separate business, hiring resources at the local account, with each account manager managing a complete income statement. While simplistic, the accounts were added up, corporate overhead applied, and it worked well for the first few years. This was also well before the explosion of computing technologies that started to tie the business world together in faster and closer ways.

Early Growth

As the industry grew, both in capability and in reach, other products were developed, other approaches to engineered solutions were invented, and the complexity of delivery (and therefore account management) expanded rapidly. More accounts came online and more resources were hired at local levels. As workload needs fluctuated at accounts, the workforce flexed to keep in sync with demand. At first, this hiring/firing cycle was offset by using temporary workers for temporary work, but complexity was also expanding and required a broader approach to both staffing and skills development. As the industry was developing new technology, a more technically skilled workforce was also evolving on the same time line.

After a few years, the company became a publicly traded corporation and continued to expand rapidly, diversified its industry base, and took on more customers for various products, all within its core competencies. In addition, productivity improvements (based on new technology and efficiencies) were achieved, and clients started requesting more and different services, including hardware changes, network administration, security management, applications development, and others. Many of these were even more temporary in nature (projects where workers with very specific skills would come and go). The ability to rapidly scale up or down was an important differentiator for providing value to clients at competitive prices. Skill sets became more differentiated, allowing the industry to possess more specific technology skills;

however, it meant that many workers on individual accounts had to rotate through assignments and locations.

Other than a core group that would stay on the account, the need was evolving for a stable of "transient" resources with increasingly diversified technical and project-management skill sets. In a natural evolution of the business model, resource pools were created that specialized in developing and maintaining specific skills within disciplines. These could then be deployed locally, regionally, or, finally, nationally. Resources were hired into resource management pools, their skills and capabilities developed and catalogued and then deployed from the pools as needed. Although this changed the basic nature of the business model, it was seen as evolutionary growth, and the logical impact on how this would be managed was not foreseen.

The company grew exponentially with the technology explosion, also bringing on disciplines from ERP applications to business process outsourcing (BPO) of various functions. While there were still accounts with the majority of workers employed at the account level, more and more accounts were made up of a core group supported by a larger group of resources assigned from resource teams. At the same time, the Internet explosion was making connectivity, security, and bandwidth available to a broader and broader set of resources, and more and more work could be done remotely. Many of the resources were still being deployed from resource pools but were seen as long-term account employees, often moving to live at the account site, yet still managed out of a centralized resource pool by skill sets. At the same time, specialized skills were required for shorter periods of time to handle short-term specialized projects, which continued to promote building resource pools. Larger proportions of account resources were now supplied from a central resource management group, and an organizational structure and management technique grew up around resource pools. Because the company reported quarterly income, costs, and margins on an aggregated basis, with little attention to lines of business, it made sense; however, the services industry was growing quickly, driven both by the explosion of technologies and by the drive for businesses to reduce costs for core functions by outsourcing various aspects of their business. The intended consequences of this structure is obvious; however, the unintended consequences will become clearer in the following sections.

Changes in Leadership

As inevitably happens, senior leadership changed, and the corporate focus changed toward differentiating among lines of business. The industry was maturing as technology provided opportunities to sell services to clients in new areas. As an aside here, it needs to be emphasized that as any organization grows beyond the ability of a core group of leaders to manage, it develops more complex management structures, such that corporate objectives can be transmitted effectively to the organization. Although there is a tendency to blame issues that arise on complexity, this is often a substitute for not knowing how to guard against unintended negative consequences of this complexity. In this case, the continued rapid growth, the introduction of skills pools, and the business models used at the account level created an environment where changes were difficult, mostly due to the fact that the approaches were incremental and impossible to change one at a time. The introduction of differentiating business lines for reporting purposes could have also introduced a redesign of the fundamental business functions to align better with these lines; however, skills pools continued to expand, creating further differentiation and clouding the lines between how resources were managed and assigned and how the business segments were reported. There are great examples of leading organizational change through transitions; however, for many business leaders this complexity leads to continued evolution without acknowledgment of the need for new business models to support the growing complexity. In other words, dramatic changes in business models are disruptive, so evolution is preferable. Not being able to fully conceptualize the issues that may arise is, at this point, a product of lack of collective knowledge of the logical relationships within the business. It is not the organization itself that creates the issues.

Continued Complexity

Each account now was given individual targets for each business segment and was often broken down yet another level. Account financials were aggregated by line of business first and then at the account level to create the overall account income statement. Resources were still acquired by a growing resource management group, which was now segmented by resource type, skill sets, and somewhat by the line of business that it supported. Leadership of resource pools was segmented by various means, some geographic, some by skills, some by the offering that they supported, but the aggregation of these resources was based on the ability to deliver the skills when needed and less by what part of the business they supported. A complex set of business rules grew up around the management and assignment of these resources.

How these resources were used at the account level, however, remained the province of individual account leaders, as in the case of project management. Although some skills and techniques are transportable between lines of business, such as IT outsourcing (ITO) or ERP, at a detail level they may be quite different. The resource management structure, however, did not provide a way to know what each assigned resource was actually doing. The design of the management structures was not intended to track these resource assignments by any methods except account statements.

Some of the business segment products tend to be sold as a comprehensive service with defined margins, while others, such as consulting, are often sold at published consulting rates, which usually contribute higher margins (sometimes by two or three times). Each account now had targets for revenue and margins by segment, with little differentiation between resources, and the habit developed of assigning resources to balance things out and achieve targets for all segments. Although the creation of resource pools and the assignment of these to account teams started out to manage resources and skills, the lack of visibility into how they were assigned at accounts would have unintended consequences later in the evolution of these programs. It is not a story of intended errors but of the unintended consequences that developed as a result of the progression of this industry and evolutionary decisions made along the way. As long as the corporation was focused on reporting total revenue and margins, this was not a problem; however, the change in reporting methods could have been cause for concern.

Corporate Restructuring

New executive leadership restructured the lines of business and incentive programs, placing further emphasis on the differentiated targets, even while much of the revenue was attributed incorrectly to other lines of business. Resource managers led their organizations based on demand for specific resources for individual accounts (short term, longer term, or permanent), which was consistent with their roles in the organization. They saw themselves as generally aligned around "systems engineering" skills that could be deployed across a whole range of different project types, and, more important, across different lines of business. At the same time, leaders were assigned to mentor the organizations to focus on differentiation of these skills and create professional progression programs based on skill and experience in more and more narrow areas of deployment. These two "evolutions" resulted in management structures and techniques that were starting to render the existing account management and reporting models inadequate. Internal reporting systems were increasingly inadequate to detect this, and the methods of coding resources and revenue at the accounts became an accepted part of the culture, not as an intended consequence, but simply because the rules and the oversight were not sensitive to the issues that the current assignment and reporting methods were creating. As long as legacy (homegrown, proprietary) applications were not sophisticated enough to report on this by providing a view where resources were coded by line of business to allow revenue to follow the resource, which would immediately point out the differences between reporting at resource levels, compared to the account level rollup, there was virtually no way for this to become visible. Most organizations have grown up by some version of this story and have different but similar examples where actual results differ from what is reported, not in the aggregate, but in an analysis of product profitability or cost attribution. The majority of organizations today have these issues left over from decades of unintended consequences.

Enter ERP and Improved Business Applications Platforms

Two things happened to all of these IT services organizations:

1. Enter ERP platforms with the ability to track information across large, complex companies and perform an analysis of results from different views.
2. A need developed to manage global accounts as global accounts, rather than as loosely integrated international collections of accounts for a single client.

A business could now use the ERP platform to look at a cross-sectional slice of total revenue and margin globally by the types of resources deployed. As businesses attempted to look at business results from this different perspective, they quickly realized that this was a problem due to the lack of consistency in the way work was recorded at the account level. This had implications for the whole business organization that had grown up over the years. The point of the example is that decisions were made over decades driven by business growth that later proved to have unintended consequences for the companies. Furthermore, the illumination of the relationships between the functional components provided by the ERP systems provided the ability to recognize, analyze, and redesign the business process to make the results of changes more predictable. This, however, is a two-edged sword because the same processes that had served so well had been fully embedded into the company and institutionalized by legal reporting, cultural and political issues, and the lack of well-developed alternative business models to migrate to. Throughout this book, we will refer back to these situations and define a methodology for program governance designed to assist organizations to manage through these changes. The salient points here are

- The issues developed as unintended consequences of actions taken to address immediate needs and were not poor designs at the time.
- These unintended consequences are now fully embedded in the organizational culture and require a different approach to resolve them.
- Not addressing the need for transformational change will lead to failure to achieve intended business benefits.

Example 2: Manufacturing and Distribution

Remember that these examples are intended to demonstrate how normal business and growth activities, exacerbated by industries that are being affected by changes in technology and customers, will end up evolving business processes and systems that become problematic. This always makes major events, such as the implementation of ERP applications, more difficult and results in the need for exceptional program governance to ensure the success of changes.

The second example is a manufacturing company making products in the printing industry. One of the characteristics of the industry at the time was that printing plates were sold in all kinds of shapes, sizes, and thicknesses to a large number of end clients (small family-owned shops). This industry, like virtually all industries associated with photo processes, has evolved to more computer-to-press technologies, and much of this description is now dated; however, the intent is to show the evolution of processes for reasons that seemed right at the time but eventually created an environment that was difficult to change. Again, as in the first example, this example is taken from a variety of sources, and some details are constructed to explain the observations in order to fill in the blanks, but the example makes the case about how things get to the point where they are difficult to change.

Early History

In the early days of the lithographic printing industry, printing was concentrated in a few printers, mostly because of the money needed to acquire equipment. There were a few different sizes of plates for different types of equipment, and with modifications, there were a number of setups that had to be customized; however, the size and diversity of the product line were limited. With larger, better-funded businesses, supplies such as plates could be ordered ahead, and the time that it took to get from the factory order to the customer was well understood—it worked. As time went by, however, printers became more ubiquitous, causing an explosion of small printers close to their customers, which resulted in further modifications to equipment and setups. This caused the number of stocked end-items to rise, but with smaller print shops, inventory orders were smaller and delivery times more critical.

Growth Breeds Complexity

Demand for shorter and shorter lead times resulted in several changes:

- More and different setups required more stocked end-items.
- Delivery times were reduced to the point where transportation time became a significant component of competition.
- An intermediate layer of distributors in local cities expanded, acting as an intermediary to the smaller print shops.

In addition, once this process started, it continued to compress demand for stock items in various setups and for faster delivery times over several years. This was also during the time in the 1980s when literature talked more about excessive costs of working capital as Manufacturing Resources Planning (MRP II) thinking caused leaner stocks to be held at distributors and customers. Competition for customers became more and more dependent on reliability, defined as an ability to get their products quickly, and the ability to switch from one vendor to another became easier as the product moved from a specialty to a commodity.

Building a Better Distribution System

As the number of printers expanded and the products became commodities, regional sales offices responded by establishing their own regional distribution centers to supply product more quickly. Each distribution center "belonged" to the regional sales manager, and it became the customer for the manufacturing plant. Its orders would be received by manufacturing and placed into a production schedule; however, the production time lines varied significantly, with the result that stock levels in regional centers grew much faster than the business they supported. In many cases, this was essentially the "Boston Beer Case" described by Peter Senge in *The Fifth Discipline*, where shortages result in allocation of stock, which results in increased orders, which results in excess demands on manufacturing, causing expansion of production output, which results in excess inventory at the distribution centers, which results in canceled orders as inventory grows.[3] Although this may have been a natural response to the supply-chain issues the company was experiencing, costs continued to grow out of proportion to business growth. For a more thorough explanation of the Boston Beer Case, *The Fifth Discipline* (Chapter 3) provides an insightful description of the law of unintended Consequences and is good reading.

Manufacturing Gets Clogged

With the perception of excess demand on manufacturing, the production organization staffed to keep up; however, new employees, long hours, and less average experience in workers resulted in some items arriving on time and others requiring expediting until so many orders were expedited, it took expediting within the expedited orders to get items to the customers on time. At the same time, back orders continued to rise, eventually peaking at $3.5M, and many items could be on back order for a month or more at a time. One of the final steps in manufacturing was cutting plates to size using large hydraulic cutters. The next remedy was that press cutters were ordered for each distribution center to be used for "emergencies." In this case, the distribution center would take a package of a larger size, open it, cut it down into the needed size, repackage it, and ship it. Despite the additional work, the lost yield on the plates, and the additional packaging materials, this initially met the need to get products to the final customers on time. Costs, however, in the form of inventory (which, of course, had to be increased to accommodate this rework department), labor, and waste increased significantly, even as the market price for the products was dropping precipitously.

The Situation at Its Worst

This is the point at which integrated systems were introduced into the mix. The situation was that sales were controlled regionally, each ordering directly on manufacturing; manufacturing was being cycled wildly as the Boston Beer Case scenario was playing out; quality was becoming worse and worse as expediting took over and inexperienced workers were introduced; and, not surprisingly, back orders continued to rise because nearly every plate that was cut down had been in stock to fill an order anticipated during the next few days. Eventually, more than half of all plates were produced, shipped to distribution centers, recut, and then shipped to customers; inventory doubled overall in the system; and sales dropped precipitously.

Resolution

Inevitably, at the point where ERP systems are introduced, scenarios such as this have occurred in any number of functions within the company. The politics and the culture have adopted intransigent positions around how to solve the issues, and most of the discussions concern whose idea to use—remember that every idea represents a functional view of both the problem and the potential solutions. Each step along this path included steps taken to address the immediate problem, and each initially resulted in improved results. Each, however, resulted in unintended consequences as a result of lack of knowledge of how integrated business processes operate.

Again, this is an example of everyone working functionally to take actions to address real issues with real solutions, and only through the illumination of the business process logic could the creation of unintended negative consequences be addressed. In this case, an integrated approach to sales forecasting, distribution, and manufacturing planning was successful in transforming how the business operated. The same challenges exist today in the vast majority of ERP implementations and are often not addressed effectively, resulting in failure to achieve intended business benefits.

 THE CHALLENGE

The salient points from these stories include

1. Things grow over the years by what were at the outset good ideas or, at least, not overtly bad ideas. These can include many different phenomena, from "not invented here" attitudes to issues of organizational size and individual contributions. Without any intent to create other problems or issues, the evolution of processes has always produced more consequences than those anticipated.
2. Leadership changes, legal status changes (private versus public), organizational structures designed to meet immediate needs continue to provide a change dynamic to any organization, which over time we label "corporate culture"—nothing earth shattering, simply the collection of managerial techniques and structures that grow over decades in any

company. The only real change is that the advent of ERP platforms is a dramatic shift in the ability to see and report across functions where numbers can be consistently applied.

3. The same structures that may serve a company well when they were established ultimately may be impediments to continued growth and progress decades later, but by then, they have become thoroughly entrenched in the politics and the culture of the organization. Everything from legal reporting to compensation incentives and promotion competition will become tied to these structures and are difficult to discuss.

4. Legal reporting (Sarbanes-Oxley) takes a look at several aspects of financial reporting to ensure that the stated financial results of the corporation accurately reflect the financial status of the company. In doing so, the audit process evaluates internal controls and process reliability to determine whether the company is meeting the standards set forth in the law. These tools have become more competent at identifying weaknesses in business process management.

5. There is a whole issue beyond legal reporting, however, that doesn't get touched by the audit process—board level enterprise risk management. Beyond simple financial analysis and evaluation techniques, it is possible to develop other statistical financial analysis documents that can point to where these structural risks and opportunities exist.

6. Discovery of these issues often occurs during the ERP implementation project, but project teams have a difficult time defining issues well enough to get resolution to highly political cultural issues at the executive level.

7. In order to ensure that these are identified and resolved, we need a wholly new and detailed process of program governance that works through high-level issues standing in the way. Essentially, we are not building a whole new organization; however, we are building an entire new mirror infrastructure that has a dramatic impact on how our corporations operate.

 SUMMARY

This chapter outlines simple examples of how things develop over time and eventually create what Chris Argyris in *Overcoming Organizational Defenses* calls the triple-blind failure to resolve them. In other words, we decide not to discuss the fact that we cannot discuss why discussions around these thorny issues cannot be successful.

If you read back over the several iterations of what ended up being an intransigent cultural process that prevents improvement, think about what happens at each stage of the evolution when you try to change the system. As the system of managing resources and assigning them to accounts evolves, as the account managers learn how to manage resources to achieve business targets, as growth targets get set that drive compensation programs at all levels, and, finally, as the business is segmented into parts that are evaluated and reported on separately, this is a story of the inability to see the organization from top to bottom. In the second example, as the industry grows, in its early development systems are established to address market needs; however, as it grows, diversifies, and ultimately converts from a specialty business to a commodity business, all of the changes are made within the functional culture of the organization without any view to the impact that it is having on the other functions. Beyond that, because each change in organizational structure was developed and implemented by the functional departments, they are committed to their solutions and to demonstrating why the continuing issues are the fault of others.

It is this final part of the story that this book suggests calls for a new approach to achieving potential business benefits from the use of ERP systems.

 NOTES

1. For more discussion of this, there are many articles available—one that is valuable is from Rob Norton titled "Unintended Consequences" and can be found at the Library of Economics and Liberty at http://www.econlib.org/library/Enc/UnintendedConsequences.html.
2. Chris Argyris, *Overcoming Organizational Defenses: Facilitating Organizational Learning* (Upper Saddle River, NJ: Prentice Hall, 1990).
3. Peter Senge, *The Fifth Discipline* (New York: Bantam Doubleday Dell Publishing Group, 1990).

2

Leadership and Change in an Integrated Business World

"By any objective measure, the amount of significant, often traumatic, change in organizations has grown tremendously over the past two decades. Although some people predict that most of the reengineering, restrategizing, mergers, downsizing, quality efforts, and cultural renewal projects will soon disappear, I think that is highly unlikely. Powerful macroeconomic forces are at work here, and these forces may grow even stronger over the next few decades. As a result, more and more organizations will be pushed to reduce costs, improve the quality of products and devices, locate new opportunities for growth, and increase productivity."

—*John Kotter*, Leading Change

INTRODUCTION

We are deluged with euphoric articles about every new business application and how it can be deployed and can make great contributions to a business. Leaders, however, continue to struggle to adopt approaches that produce tangible, measurable, and reliable Return on Investment. The most pervasive of these applications are broadly known as Enterprise Resource Planning (ERP) applications.

It is also a commonly held belief that this failure to produce results is simply a failure of leadership, when often failures are the product of a more widely spread lack of process understanding within the executive team. How many times have you heard the explanation for resistance to changes being implemented as "having to do it the XYZ (SAP, Oracle, or other) way?" when it is actually the result of a logical business process that prevents some designs. It is also frequently the lack of understanding of the work required to integrate new business processes into existing cultural and political environments where failures appear and, if not effectively addressed, become reality.

 THE UNIVERSE OUTSIDE, THE UNIVERSE WITHIN

It may be too many parts of the organization changing at the same time whose interactions are poorly understood, or it may be a lack of ability to manage the organization as a whole organism, rather than as a collection of the pieces. Prior to the introduction of ERP programs, IT applications supporting departments evolved slowly and functionally, using interfaces to connect pieces to one another. In this scenario, functional departments designed transactions to meet their own needs and left it to IT to figure out how to interface them with other parts of the business. Although disputes occurred, the system evolved slowly enough that it was somewhat contained. Many of these "interfaces" were really extensive programs to overcome differences in data models or definitions, but they kept things in some sort of order. Furthermore, it did not require leaders to understand relationships among pieces or to follow a set design approach to make them fit.

While this approach reduced friction and disruption, it also supported the development of dysfunctional processes, as described in the last chapter. In order to reverse this lack of knowledge, either more of the mechanics behind business processes must be understood by individual leaders or a method of dealing with the issues raised must be established. With the likelihood of the first of these quite remote and likely even counterproductive, we will propose a different managed approach to guiding the change process.

Many analogies could be made to illustrate this point because the illumination of knowledge of logical systems is universal in promoting learning. Let's compare the arrival of ERP systems and their effect on the development of new understanding of logical relationships among business functions to the development of powerful telescopes and their impact on the expanding knowledge of our universe. As telescopes were invented and became more powerful over the centuries, we have been able to look deeper into space and discover new relationships in our cosmos, which has changed the way we view our universe and our theories of how it works. The universe didn't change; our knowledge of the processes at work, however, did.

The same is true of business process knowledge. ERP programs have not created "altered states" in business processes, so much as they have illuminated the logical relationships between business functions and components. By doing this, they have provided us with an opportunity to understand more about the unintended consequences that occur when we take actions in one function without fully understanding all of the impacts that will occur as natural logical consequences elsewhere in our business (kind of like the theory that the sun revolves around the earth). The form that business processes in the ERP system takes is more a product of discovering these logical relationships than it is any reordering of the business universe. Deeper understanding of natural relationships necessarily changes the way we view business processes, and leadership functions must evolve to accept this and adopt approaches to manage this process.

 ## THE JOURNEY

First, however, let's start with a definition of leadership. Leadership journeys have evolved over the years by analyzing successes to discover what seems to have worked and what has not. John Kotter developed his approach to leadership and change management principles and tools that started with his book *A Force for Change: How Leadership and Management Differ* and has followed that book with several others about leadership principles in change programs.[1] We will adopt Kotter's basic model of leadership as the starting point for this discussion. Kotter talks about the three components of effective leadership as being able to

1. Develop a compelling vision for the organization.
2. Align organizational leaders to the collective vision.
3. Motivate and inspire the organization.

Kotter's second principle requires the leader to align his or her staff with the vision that has been created. There is an assumption implicit in this that the leadership team has sufficient skills to execute its functions in support of this vision, both individually and collectively. This assumption, however, is often incorrect when it pertains to the relationship between business processes and the IT applications that define and institutionalize them. Although this may seem like artificially adding another element to Kotter's basic model, we believe that this is far from the truth. There are some business visions that may not rely heavily on IT changes in order to achieve them, but it is difficult to think of any. Virtually everything that we can dream up to change in a business requires extensive reworking of one part or another of IT applications, and this just becomes more complex in an ERP environment. This is a fundamental principle of how you understand a business, what James Milojkovic called a contextual principle, as described in the Introduction. As discussed, his model incorporates current learning models for "action" and "thinking" challenges and goes on to add "contextual" learning as a necessary addition to the better-understood ones.[2] This requires knowledge of mental models or paradigms that frame the way we have learned to interpret our universe, just as in the previously mentioned astronomy example. For instance, if your basic belief in how businesses operate is functional, and you believe that optimizing your function will automatically optimize others or at least not create unintended consequences greater than the benefit you gain, then the role that the leadership team plays is quite different from what is needed. If, conversely, you believe that business process designs must be developed, tested, and evaluated across all functions affected and the best solution for the organization be chosen, the role of the leadership team changes significantly.

If you are going to transform customer-facing programs, a leader depends on managers who are experienced with high-performing sales organizations. You would not, for example, elect to put an expert with 30 years of experience in accounting in charge of designing and implementing a new sales organization or market approach or the other way around. An organizational leader first selects experienced and competent people to put into key positions.

It is possible to align a leadership team to a vision and create great enthusiasm for the goals of the organization and still not ensure that the team contains all of the knowledge necessary to resolve issues. Sometimes it is not just enthusiasm but the existence of all of the necessary skills that results in success or failure. While Kotter goes on to talk about managing as being different from leadership, the leadership model implies that at the outset, the team is competent to deal with the challenges. The relationship between business and IT leaders is too often overlooked, particularly when neither understands the role of integrated business processes in determining business results.

In most organizations today, the IT function is led by outstanding technologists, which is certainly necessary, considering the explosion of new technologies. A problem, however, has occurred as the role of technology has evolved not only as a technical function but also as a key business function, two totally different sets of experience. Attendant to this last component, this book will discuss the lack of cross-functional understanding of how integrated business applications define and support business processes, as well as the actions to be taken to create competency within the organization to deal with issues that arise as the organization embarks on extensive changes to business processes. This competency does not exist to any great degree in many organizations today and consequently must be created in order to be successful in executing programs to achieve the vision, whatever that might be. Chapter 10 describes a governance model to oversee both the business process revolution and the continuous change programs necessary to accomplish this.

 ## THE EVOLUTION OF INTEGRATED PROGRAMS FOR CONTINUOUS IMPROVEMENT

In the early 1980s, the era of quality programs started in industries in the United States. Drs. Deming and Juran would correctly say that this actually started at the end of World War II in Japan, as they were advising Japanese corporate leaders on how to improve reliability and efficiency in their industrial complex while the Japanese recovered from the war.[3] However, the introduction of these programs effectively came to the United States 30 years later. These quality programs introduced many new concepts, from distinguishing the difference between "Cost of Compliance" and "Cost of Noncompliance" to the use of statistical methods to determine variability in processes both in manufacturing and in administration.[4] This has continued with the introduction of Six Sigma, lean manufacturing, Lean

Six Sigma, and many more. All of these programs brought tools that allow us to better understand logical relationships within a business. More and more, we became better at evaluating effectiveness based on reliability and consistency. As well, these tools help identify variability in processes and determine causes to be managed through tighter controls. Some had mathematical tools, others employee involvement, but all proposed steps that should be taken to implement their programs. At the same time, IT applications development made significant progress in designing tools to be used to support business changes. The merging of these streams that came together in the late 1980s produced the start of the ERP revolution. These are not individual programs working with an aspect of business design but are a broader look at logical relationships to eliminate negative unintended consequences. It requires the alignment of all aspects of managing the complexities of business change in order to be successful. Quality programs are simply one tool that is available to help illuminate logical relationships within business processes, so that they can be addressed.

A DEEPER LOOK INTO INTEGRATION

Yet perhaps this is too simply stated. It is really much more difficult to explain how to conceptualize the potential of business improvement as you create a vision for the organization. Furthermore, once a vision of benefits and a path are set, lack of comprehensive education and experience with how IT applications define business processes to achieve that vision often cause program failures. With outstanding executives in organizations that are used to success, this seems counterintuitive, and yet, since the dawn of integrated business applications in the early 1990s (when they first became practical for the majority of businesses), billions of dollars have been spent on implementing them, and we still have failure to get them implemented, or businesses fail to achieve business potential even when new systems have been installed. This book will take leadership principles from Kotter and others, apply them to leading change in large organizations, and demonstrate why these efforts often fail to achieve anticipated results.

MRP II COMES TO THE MAINSTREAM

Some years ago, while introducing MRP II principles to a manufacturing organization, I hired a consultant to train a large number of people on MRP principles. One day while walking through the plant, discussing how it was organized and managed, the consultant suddenly grabbed me by the arm and, leading me to the other side of an aisle, explained that he was afraid that I would trip over a "gold nugget" on the floor. All I could see was a work station and a pallet of WIP (work in process) stacked beside it. He asked me what the pallet was doing there, and I indicated that it was waiting for the worker to complete her current job and get started on this next job. It might sit there for a couple of days before it was needed. Looking around the shop floor, we could see piles of material in every direction that were also "waiting to be worked on." There was nearly a million dollars' worth of inventory just sitting, mostly because it gave comfort to the workers that their next job was there waiting for them, despite the fact that this structural million dollars of inventory was costing the company somewhere between $100K and $250K (depending on how you calculate cost of inventory) annually, with no tangible benefit. With this relationship between inventory and planning exposed, we looked at the rest of the shop floor and warehouse. We discovered $27M of inventory stranded in one place or another, providing no tangible business benefits (a cost to the organization of $3M to $7M annually).

Illumination can come from many directions, some not intuitive; however, anything that reveals logical relationships can prove valuable. Decades ago, DuPont created a program called STOP (Stop to Observe Program) that was instrumental in making that company the safety leader of the chemical industry. The concept was simple—when you enter a room, stop and keenly observe what is happening around you, based on having prepared yourself for what to expect—and comes from the audit principles of:

- Understand the regulation, rule, or idea you are trying to evaluate.
- Create or understand the rules or policies that have been created to deliver that result.
- Think through what you would observe if the business processes were effective in complying with that policy.
- Plan to look for examples that would indicate failures to comply with policies.
- STOP.
- Take action based on initial observations, understanding that failure to comply is an indication of failure and is not usually accidental.

This STOP principle or program applies to nearly everything that we are discussing here and will play heavily in Chapter 4 on "Return on Investment." Process units out of control and unstable, piles of inventory not being worked on, excessive back orders, and, finally, loss of customers or suppliers are all symptoms of problems that can be detected by these methods and targeted to be addressed by the programs described in this book. Leaders must continuously be trained to take opportunities to see and understand the logical relationships that define business results.

THE MOVE TO IT-RELATED APPLICATIONS SOLUTIONS

Now, let's move forward a decade or more and follow the natural progression of how tools create knowledge of logical relationships, thereby allowing for improvement opportunities. MRP I, developed by James Orlicky and others in the late 1950s, was a parts planning system where knowledge of time-phased demand and materials used to build sales items could be utilized to predict demand from suppliers.[5] MRP II took these concepts and incorporated them into a "closed loop planning system" that included planning relationships from sales forecasting through parts ordering.[6] Actually, starting in the early 1970s, but really becoming viable in the late 1980s, MRP II became a component of ERP, where financial planning was an integral part of the logistics and resources planning processes. In doing so, the relationships between diverse functions become entangled into cross-functional business process designs. The push for the evolution of ERP from MRP and financial planning tools became part of the drive from business applications developers to capture, dissect, and analyze massive amounts of data, requiring more understanding of the relationships between functions.

As time passed, more and more components were developed. IT technology, MRP II, audit protocols, and others were starting to converge. To deal with cross-functional relationships, concepts of business process reengineering were developed in the early 1990s, led by Michael Hammer and James Champy.[7] Closely following was the evolution of management consulting into a new industry segment selling transformational, rather than incremental, change with the promise of producing transformational benefits. During the following two decades, tools ranging from business process mapping and design toolsets to entire business process management software suites (Metastorm and many others) were created to support a systematic analysis of current states, planning for improvement programs, and managing organizational change.[8] It took a decade for many of these to be "married" to logical approaches incorporated into ERP systems, and today, we still find camps that focus on one aspect of the issue or the other, both in consulting companies and in executive leadership teams. Often there is little understanding that the two must be incorporated into a single program, managed jointly and not competitively. As all of these approaches, programs, and toolsets merge into one business transformation stream, a number of significant needs become obvious. The next section of this chapter deals with these needs and how they affect the gap between organizational needs and common practice today.

All of this implies a cognitive change in how business executives think about their business and how it is managed. This could be an attribute of a leader who is conversant with all of these programs and tools. Directing this process himself or herself, however, could be counterproductive by taking the leader away from more important roles that he or she plays. The alternative is to establish a program-governance approach to support the organization during the transformation that may become a permanent part of creating and managing a culture of continuous improvement.

 ## LEADERS AND THE LEADERSHIP GAP

The leadership needs for business planning include

- A business must establish a vision for how these capabilities can be used to produce business results.
- The leadership team must be aligned to that vision, including integration skill sets.
- Tools must be identified to support the transformation.
- Leaders must understand how these tools and the vision align.
- There must evolve a shared understanding of logical relationships in the business.

With this background and approach, it is easy to see that leaders who are able to understand the operational level in each discipline and approach, as well as the toolsets, are in short supply. Business leaders generally gain their positions by excellence in one or two disciplines at most, as well as through their ability to work with others to achieve corporate objectives. Thinking back to Kotter's three components—create a vision, align people to that vision, and then motivate/inspire them to develop programs to execute that vision— works well as long as the collective knowledge, experience, and collaborative relationships of the leadership team are sufficient. A problem arises, however, when this level of understanding doesn't exist, a common situation today.

We have to recognize that cross-functional methods of viewing, analyzing, and correcting business issues have evolved only during the last 20 years. Most of this collaborative understanding came only in the last 5 or 10 years, and for most of that time, the resolution of issues such as this has been relegated to IT leaders and considered a technical issue. As will be discussed in Chapter 3, the majority of questions that have been asked of IT leadership either have been of a technical nature (thereby recognizing their traditional role) or have been dissected by function where the challenge has been more of prioritizing requests, rather than creating cross-functional solutions. For a better understanding of this principle, let's use a real-life example of this phenomenon.

I was asked to visit with the CIO of a mid-size oil company to discuss how the company was using its ERP asset. In his office, I was introduced to three people, all of whom were obviously less than pleased that I was there—the CIO and two IT directors. After exchanging pleasantries, we started to talk about their ERP system and the work they were doing, but the conversation was interrupted. The CIO explained to me in confrontational terms that his company had controlled its IT budget to 1.1 percent of revenue, and that was the lowest in their industry. It was obvious that the "vision" for this organization was to find ways to reduce the amount of money that it spent on IT as a singular objective.

The premise I had been presented with and on which the visit was based was that the organization was having a difficult time using its ERP applications to achieve its expected Return on Investment and that it needed help. Getting beyond the obviously poorly prepared meeting, I asked the CIO to help me understand whether they were proud of that statement or ashamed of it—admittedly an aggressive approach; however, directly to the issue. Surely, someone in the organization had to understand the relationship between business processes and business applications included in the ERP software they had deployed. I went on to explain that to take an extremely expensive—and potentially the most powerful—asset that the corporation had (based on its potential to create a Return on Investment for the business) and suboptimize the ability to use it for that end was something that they should be trying to reverse. They needed to listen to their business partners, help define a business case based on Return on Investment, set this into their objectives, and increase spending, while insisting that they achieve the Return on Investment. In other words, the ERP platform was a tool to produce improved business results potentially many times greater than the investment.

My meeting did not last long, but the experience I gained that day has stuck with me ever since. The problem at this company was clearly a matter of what its vision was. Company leaders had created the vision that they would control costs into improving business results. A more effective vision would have been to develop a program that allowed projects to be developed based on potential business improvements and supported by effective Return on Investment cases; however, that would have to be inclusive of a shift in how they viewed the relationship between the IT applications and business processes—a contextual change in Dr. Milojkovic's model. Furthermore, a base case would have to be developed and agreed on and projects managed toward achieving those goals, and overall profitability of the company would improve based on creating greater efficiencies in the operations and the markets that they served. This company continues today to be considered a low-cost producer with reasonable profitability but limited perspective or vision. It also defines a collective knowledge gap that won't be closed without acknowledgment of the need.

Vision

If the first task of a leader is to create a vision for his or her organization, it stands to reason that this process must be based on reasonable knowledge of the mechanics of what he or she is trying to create. For example, if the vision is to become the market leader in a particular business segment, based on inventing and bringing to market the most creative products in the segment, the vision has to be based on knowledge of the market being serviced, knowledge of the products being sold and used in that market, understanding the research capabilities of the organization, and having confidence in the ability of the team that either exists or will exist to achieve the vision.

Now, let's consider the vision to create an IT transformation program using existing and emerging technologies to improve business processes, such that the company becomes the lowest-cost, highest-quality producer in the market—and will do so by creating a Return on Investment stream greater than the investment in the technology. In the latter case, the vision must be based on understanding how business processes produce whatever the business results are going to be, how to design business processes, and how the IT business applications can be deployed to achieve these benefits, as well as on the cost structures of the business, the political and cultural structures of the organization at the executive staff level, and many other issues. The point is that in the case of IT-led transformation, the odds are significantly against having an individual who has achieved the CEO/COO role in an organization having had direct experience leading to this knowledge. It is therefore imperative that leaders find the combined skills in their staff members who can create a business case and approach that allows this vision to be achieved or, alternatively, to install a governance program to manage the cross-functional design and implementation process.

Staff groups are made up of executives who have risen through functional responsibilities in which they are expert and have demonstrated outstanding performance and results but who depend on other executives to contribute knowledge outside of their experience. When it comes to IT, this is where the concept of hybrid resources, described by Peter G. W. Keen in his book *Shaping the Future*, comes in.[9] These are leaders who have taken assignments outside of their primary career paths to gain knowledge and experience with other functions and the relationships among them. It could be an operations executive taking a corporate position in quality management, a controller taking a position in strategic planning, or many more. Or, it could be a functional leader taking a role in the IT organization, leading technical resources to produce applications solutions to resolve business problems. This has long been a challenge for organizations where career paths are managed more by mentors and sponsors, and where corporate memory spans rarely survive changes in leadership. Fortunate individuals are those who accept these broadening assignments for a period of time and are able to move back before the organization forgets what was intended. This process has served to limit those who are willing to take on these enrichment opportunities.

Further issues are having the self-confidence in getting outside of one's comfort zone, being able to develop the ability and skills to perform well in different functions, and overcoming the fear that the broadening experience might become career limiting and not career enhancing. The point is that the development of this kind of program and the ability to manage leaders through it over time is uncertain and perhaps not even likely. The likelihood of the development of hybrid managers in a business is highly dependent on the learning that is encouraged within the organization and on the logical relationships that define business results.

First among the areas limited by this is IT, because it has always been a mostly technical function where academic education and technical study have been necessary to do well. Since the introduction of integrated ERP systems in the early 1990s, however, this has become less true, although there is still and will always be a highly technical component. No doubt, there is a need for highly technical and creative individuals to manage the technology side of systems, but today, business value is more often delivered by how well the integrated business processes are analyzed, designed, and implemented, and this value is at least equally dependent on business process knowledge that lies within the functional departments.

What Does a Leader Do?

Getting back to the initial question—how do leaders develop a vision that is based on knowledge and concepts that they know well but that also requires significant understanding that has not been part of their background or education? From the leader's perspective, this is really the question. Even good leaders, who have been able to develop and communicate strong visions about markets, products, outreach, and other important aspects of the business, falter when it comes to conceptualizing a vision around optimizing internal operations and cost structures of their business. Instead, they tend to turn the responsibility over to the CIO or IT directors, whose role has always been to keep up with the technology and its applications, and who are not fully embedded in the business, nor are they looked to for this vision. Worse yet, a cost-reduction program may end up being driven by need without knowledge.

With the growing explosion of technological capability, leadership is becoming even more difficult. If you attend a technical conference supported by any leading technology company, you will be deluged by incredibly impressive new tools, functions, hardware, and capabilities that can be added to your existing systems or the ones you are in the process of implementing. This "cool tools" phenomenon, where the tools are presented in such a way that they really excite the mind and stir thoughts of the potential they represent, is pervasive, as well as persuading. This should certainly not be a surprise— technology companies don't gain respect and share price in the market by crowing about what they developed or sold yesterday, nor should they. Their job in industry is to develop technology, tools, and capabilities that corporations can use to expand markets, improve efficiencies, and succeed in their results.

What tends to get lost in this, however, is the value that can be achieved by focusing on business processes that determine business results, whether this is in the outside market or internal efficiencies. If the current tools for in-memory computing, cloud delivery, and mobility can improve speed and efficiency in a corporation, just imagine what would be possible if the business applications the enterprise operates on were optimized to produce improved business results. If customer relationship management (CRM) front-end sales support systems were optimally integrated with manufacturing, distribution, and planning systems, think how much more effective the mobility applications and ad hoc queries would become.

The point is the need to separate capabilities from business process efficiencies and develop a hybrid function that will always relate new tools back to real needs. Poor information that is created and delivered faster to the user is only faster, never better, and often produces further negative unintended consequences. Furthermore, many users don't have the experience to know what to ask for or how. This "lack of information" is often the result of the needed data not being collected at the point of origin, mostly because data elements were never created or captured in the transactional process. When basic data doesn't exist, the futility of getting this to the user faster becomes apparent.

In a typical example, an organization was having serious issues with "getting reports" out of its ERP system. The belief that the system was not capable of producing necessary reports was pervasive throughout the organization, to the point that nearly everyone had his or her own spreadsheets to organize and analyze data, which people then fed back into the ERP system. The answer proposed was to implement a data warehouse (part of the ERP platform), demonstrate it to the user community and then ask people to figure out how to use it. The challenge, faced by many organizations today, is that before you can effectively use "cool tools" to resolve business problems, you need business leaders to define both the problem they are trying to solve and the information that they need to properly make business decisions in the future. Today's "cool tools" provide support for nearly anything business leaders can come up with; however, the solution may not be as easy as a new tool and may even require going back into the base systems to create new data elements or add fields to transactions in order to capture information needed to produce the analysis that will help move the business forward. Either existing leaders have to increase their overall knowledge in the workforce to relate more effectively to the issue, or they need to create a support function to manage this process.

Align Employees to the Vision

Even if leaders get past this point, they find it difficult to articulate the vision to functional subordinates and align these subordinates to work together to achieve the company's vision. All of this must be done, of course, within the political and cultural organization that manages the company. It is a common experience to talk with executive teams who understand the vision and articulate it very well, and then to talk with mid-level managers who can recite the vision but indicate that senior leadership talks the vision but doesn't understand the actions necessary to realize it. It is this necessity to understand the opportunity, conceptualize the vision, articulate the vision to subordinates, align different functions and interests to support the vision, and work through organizational challenges caused by cross-functional design decisions in a highly political environment that makes this so difficult. This difficulty nearly always results in not achieving results that are available through the opportunity provided by ERP software.

To further complicate the issue, education in business schools on these principles has only now started to be incorporated into programs, so it is necessary to find other ways to get through this learning process to achieve the Return on Investment that is possible. We like to solve difficult issues by "training," but this issue is much more pervasive than can be addressed by a simple seminar, and it will take decades before cross-functional leadership can be incorporated into university business school programs, both undergraduate and graduate. It requires leaders to change their thought processes to recognize the integrated business components and realize that improvement opportunities lie in the relationship between the pieces—a contextual or paradigm shift. Consequently, as part of the role of leadership, it is necessary to create an integrated approach to resolving these issues, and education in the logic that ERP can illuminate must become a key component of those programs. If this is done effectively, the process of motivating and inspiring the organization becomes easier.

SUMMARY

Chapter 1 outlined how large enterprises evolve over time, resulting in the political and cultural structures becoming dysfunctional, entrenched, and intransigent. Leadership, as part of the visioning process, must develop a view of an organization where these barriers to improvement are reduced through education. Going back to Deming in *Out of the Crisis*, we need to stop pointing the blame at "those bad executives (or workers, in his words)," while analyzing the cultural and political processes and creating a function that can help improve the decision-making process over time. This will leave the business organization with a cadre of executives who, collectively, have sufficient knowledge and experience to produce positive business results. A path to achieving this is described in the governance process presented in Part III of this book.

NOTES

1. John Kotter, *A Force for Change: How Leadership and Management Differ* (New York: Free Press, 1990).
2. James Milojkovic, Knowledge Passion, Inc., http://www.knowledgepassion.com/KPvisitor/KPvWelcome.html.
3. W. Edwards Deming, *Out of the Crisis* (Cambridge: Massachusetts Institute of Technology, Center for Advanced Engineering Study, 1982, 1986).
4. Philip B. Crosby, *Quality Is Free: The Art of Making Quality Certain* (New York: McGraw Hill, 1979); Deming, *Out of the Crisis.*
5. James Orlicky, *Material Requirements Planning* (New York: McGraw-Hill, 1975).
6. Oliver Wight, *Manufacturing Resource Planning: MRP II: Unlocking America's Productivity Potential*, rev. ed. (New York: John Wiley & Sons, 1995).
7. Michael Hammer and James Champy, *Re-engineering the Corporation: A Manifesto for Business Revolution* (New York: Harper Business Essentials, 1993).
8. Geary A. Rummler and Alan P. Brache, *Improving Performance, How to Manage the White Space on the Organization Chart* (San Francisco: Jossey-Bass, 1990); August-Wilhelm Scheer, *ARIS: Business Process Modeling* (Berlin: Springer-Verlag, 1999, 2000).
9. Peter G. W. Keen, *Shaping the Future* (Cambridge, MA: Harvard Business School Press, 1991).

CHAPTER THREE

A Historical Business Perspective of ERP

"Senior business executives lack a well-established management process for taking charge of IT. Business managers consequently have not developed the kind of experience and expertise in IT that they have in finance, human resources, and accounting."

—*Peter G. W. Keen*, Shaping the Future

 INTRODUCTION

Having looked at how some organizations have evolved over the years and the problems this has created, and having considered how leadership needs to create expertise in the executive team to deal with the cultural and political issues that resulted, let us now take a look at the enterprise applications platforms and how they themselves have evolved over the years.

As organizations have evolved, the need for leaders to develop knowledge of how they work and how to effectively use them to achieve business objectives has been obvious. However, little has been accomplished to acknowledge this need and develop approaches to manage the challenges effectively. It has been suggested that knowledge of the new systems and how they define and institutionalize business processes and results could as easily have evolved as a business leadership skill.

For our purposes, the discussion focuses on the role of IT and how it has evolved over the decades. We do this by reflecting on the evolution of the class of business software that comprises Enterprise Resource Planning (ERP) applications. Although the time line of this story is reasonably accurate, variations of a few years one way or the other would not change the overall conclusions or present different approaches for businesses to regain lost Return on Investment opportunities, nor would more technical details affect the outcome or conclusions of this discussion. Virtually every article, blog, marketing brochure, and consulting presentation having to do with the selection, design, implementation, enhancement, and maintenance of ERP systems will concentrate, nearly exclusively, on the technical aspects of the product and what amazing things it is capable of doing. This book takes a look at this capability from the perspective of the business and business results and talks about the extraordinary potential each generation of ERP systems has provided and how relatively little of the potential has actually been achieved.

When examining the path that the introduction, expansion, and utilization of ERP systems has taken since ERP systems became viable for most businesses in the early 1990s, one finds a clear evolutionary path in the development, the deployment, the methods used, and the evolution of the amount and types of knowledge desirable for business leaders. For historical purposes, an earlier start in this chronology will be discussed, but the mass adoption of integrated enterprise systems basically started about 1990. This movement required IT departments and workers to adjust to new realities in their relationship with business partners, but today's discussion will argue that business and IT leadership have not kept up with this transition in roles. There are many reasons for this. A key one is failure on the part of business leaders to understand that the new technologies require new approaches to the design and execution of business processes. This discussion makes the point that IT leadership has lost and continues to lose an opportunity to redefine its relationship to business and become business leaders using technology, rather than technical leaders who supply tools but not business process design leadership. To a great degree, IT continues in a support role, while IT leadership's knowledge of the new systems could provide the keys to unlock potential benefits.

During the stages discussed here, responsibility for the design, implementation, and use of the new systems has changed and continues to change, predictably providing a clear view of the future that has implications for organizations depending on these applications. We are in the middle of another (or continuing) shift in who uses the system, what they use it for, and who does the analysis. This ultimately will determine how the programs will evolve to ensure the capture of business benefits. This discussion will identify stages of development most have experienced during the last four decades and will provide a view of the transition that is coming in the next few years.

 ## LEGACY SYSTEMS (1960–1970/1990)

Until the introduction of ERP systems in the early 1970s—or when they became available to a larger number of companies in the 1990s—enterprise systems (not ERP, just the applications an enterprise operated with) evolved slowly and by business function. More often than not, they replaced repetitive and record-keeping types of activities with a more automated or accurate collection process. The first of these were financial systems, primarily general ledger, to replace handwritten ledgers kept by accountants. However, at about the same time, the automation of logistics functions started with the advent of MRP I (Material Requirements Planning) concepts developed in the early 1960s. MRP concepts were just that and often were done from tub files where a Bill of Materials (BOM) for an assembly would be retrieved from the file, an assemblies order would be created and posted to the inventory card for that part, and component demand would be entered and subtracted from the appropriate tub file cards. This expanded the use of concepts such as reorder points, blanket orders, and many more of the tools used to get control of manufacturing floors and inventories.

During the 1960s, more single-function systems were developed in customer service, finance (including accounts payable, accounts receivable, and asset management), MRP with the advent of the concept of MRP II (Manufacturing Resources Planning) to expand manufacturing process logic to include capacity planning, master production scheduling, and many more. During this time, IT applications departments were primarily aligned around a few technical skills (programming languages, mostly), and a typical worker would learn and support a couple of functional areas for many years. A COBOL programmer working in general ledger would see that skill as a likely career path and would align himself or herself with the enterprise accounting functions. Programs could be complex within the function but generally did not require knowledge of, or sensitivity to, functions outside of the one in which the person worked. User departments would think of a change to help further improve their internal processes and would ask for the changes, and the IT group would program, test, and implement. It was appropriate to consider that IT was mostly technical. Few, if any, functional business people would take IT courses as part of their education, and IT graduates were trained in their field but generally did not have any business education, to speak of. This seemed to make sense at the time.

IT'S ALL ABOUT THE BACK OFFICE: GETTING A SINGLE VERSION OF THE TRUTH (1970–1990)

In the early 1970s, a group of IBM engineers proposed to integrate all of these functions into a single application, where the logical implications of each action taken in a business were automatically and, for the most part simultaneously, posted to each of the areas affected. This was the origin of integrated business systems, known today as ERP, and was the concept that resulted in the founding of SAP. For the first time, a quantity of inventory that the inventory control system showed as in stock could be automatically multiplied by the standard cost stored in an accounting record (actually, an accounting view of a master data record for the material), and stored in the general ledger, at the same time. For the first time, there would be agreement between what inventory records showed and what accounting showed. Now, there was a single version of the truth.

IT workers continued to work within their functions, learned new skills required by the new systems, and added other programming skills to their resumes. With limited functionality, however, emphasis remained on defining relatively easy relationships between functions. The need for higher-level cross-functional integration design skills was only starting to be hinted at. Beyond basic integration, proprietary programming was still done by IT groups working exclusively with their functional partners. The touch and feel for programs were much the same, being delivered in a mainframe environment; nevertheless, this was the start of integration. For IT leadership during this time, other than learning new technical skills and continuing to support their functions, the work required was much what they had grown up with— mostly technical and requiring little real business or cross-functional business process knowledge—but the seeds were sown.

IMPROVING THE BUSINESS (1990–2000)

Flash forward to the early 1990s, however, and things really started to change. Computer technology had now advanced from the "data center" delivering everything onto the desktop. By the late 1980s, word processors, spreadsheets, desktop database programs, and many other user programs had been created. It was now possible to engage end users in the process of designing and operating the business and how to support it. Full realization of the potential and pitfalls, however, did not come along with the advances in technology. With this proliferation, something else occurred. Suddenly, all workers could have their own version of the truth by creating a spreadsheet or a database, built on their own process and logic, which could prove "conclusively" that their version was accurate, creating chaos in the management process. It also, however, evolved very quickly into an "everyone for himself" environment, with some of the creations becoming new functional business processes or work tools, while rarely communicating with other functions or departments.

Network capabilities also improved and expanded, and new concepts such as e-mail on a smart desktop computer were developed. With these exploding new technologies, the concept of client server architecture was also developed during the 1980s and provided a platform for ERP packages to exploit making integrated systems more available and useful to end users and more affordable to companies. This was the start of moving these programs from the mainframe to the desktop. The available functionality, fully integrated, was also expanding very quickly. Yet this functionality and integration were still in the back office, as the efforts were to get all of the logically interconnected functions integrated in one ERP application. This included all of the traditional financial, logistics, and human resource (HR) functions. One important side effect of this explosive expansion of integrated functionality and the creation of platforms that would make this available to a much larger group of companies was that the technology created a shift in the skills needed in both the IT and the business community. Yet this shift was not well understood or accepted at the time. Just as in the development of any new capability, it takes time for the users of that technology to understand how to use it effectively.

Coincidentally, this was also the time that concepts of business process reengineering (BPR) were being developed by Michael Hammer and James Champy in their book *Re-engineering the Corporation*.[1] Concepts of reengineering business processes with a move toward (?) integrated IT applications were an either/or decision to many, mostly because it affected the sequence of activities. At the same time that IT applications were imposing stricter master data and organizational concepts in order to achieve integration, business process management proponents were recommending that business processes should be designed based exclusively on what the business saw as optimal to meet the needs of customers. Remember that this was 10 years into U.S. businesses adopting quality programs to achieve closeness with customers and was a natural extension of that concept. The theory did not include fitting BPR designs into the integration logic of the ERP platform. This resulted in large amounts of unnecessary investment, as companies continued to create proprietary functional programs by modifying the ERP package. This was as much due to the lack of experienced consultants who could create clever solutions as it was to businesses not having the ability to think through IT-delivered business processes and how to use them to deliver equivalent business results. By the early 2000s, Dr. Hammer had come around to a more hybrid approach to making business process decisions between fitting needs into the ERP applications and developing proprietary functionality. This was mostly through the development of technology that was making the platforms more open to outside integration.

From a skills standpoint, this should have been a key opportunity for businesses to take advantage of these capabilities; however, not much happened. This was perhaps because of the race to overcome potential Y2K issues, perhaps due to a suddenly high demand for experienced consultants, or perhaps due to the business process management versus ERP dispute. After all, it is hard to find 10 years of experience when the technology has only been in existence for 5. For whatever reason, not much was done during this decade to change the knowledge level or relationships within either the business or the IT community that could bridge the gulf. Unfortunately, the quote from Peter G. W. Keen at the start of this chapter remains true today in too many cases.

The skills to design an ERP business process, configure and test the solution, and implement the software were still viewed as a technical exercise, one that IT workers were academically better prepared to support, as opposed to accountants, logistics, sales, and HR employees, who better understood business processes. The need for IT workers to expand their education in order to understand business processes and work on design issues between departments was not addressed either by universities or the ERP vendors. One must remember, IT workers had always supported one or a couple of functions at most. While the same is true for business education, the perception was that IT would just bridge the knowledge gap and allow business leaders to ignore these issues. The fact is, this change to integrated systems was a landmark shift in the overall level of knowledge and skill required to achieve the business benefits from both IT and business leadership. Although it was relatively easy to demonstrate on paper how implementation of the new business processes could drive business benefits, actually getting the process designed and accepted became a daunting task. The IT group still required a high level of technical skills in order to perform configuration and testing, but as the number of qualified resources increased late in the 1990s, the need shifted to people who understood functionally how the software worked and also understood the business.

Going further, even if IT workers understood the business, the traditional view of their role didn't provide credibility within the business, which certainly lessened the incentives to broaden their knowledge. Conversely, business leaders failed to understand that it was they who should have the responsibility to design and implement new business processes, while depending on the IT group to deliver technical details. Michael Doane, a well-known author and industry analyst, believes that the people who should actually be doing the configuration are the business people, not the IT workers.[2] His reasoning is that it is easier to teach business experts to do configuration, with help and guidance, than it is to have programmers learn all they need to know about business processes across functions. It is an interesting point, and the true answer is probably that business leaders need to accept the responsibility for the design of their business processes across functions and have the IT workers still do the actual configuration. What seems to be unquestionable, however, is that IT leadership had the opportunity to assume a leadership role in learning how to successfully design, implement, and support changes in their businesses, but, for the most part, it did not happen.

It is also true that the business school community, which could have been developing academic programs to address this need, both undergraduate and graduate, did not start to do so with any volume until at least a decade later. There were certainly courses included in the curriculum; however, concentrations focused on designing and using IT business applications to derive business benefits and how to manage this process have lagged behind even today. Nevertheless, the failure of business leadership, including IT, during those years has continued to create problems and underperforming ERP systems in the subsequent years. Unfortunately, this story isn't going to get better for some time.

THE BUSINESS SUITE: ENRICHING THE FUNCTIONALITY (1996–2005)

With the basics of the back-office integration engine well established, ERP vendors turned their attention to functionally richer front-office programs that were being developed by a variety of other vendors. These programs were CRM (customer relationship management), SCM (supply chain management), SRM (supplier relationship management), HCM (human capital management), and PLM (product life-cycle management). Now it was not only necessary to work through cross-functional issues at the integration point (ERP), it was also necessary to include business processes from outside the core functions the company connected to, such as customers, suppliers, supply chain partners, human capital functions (recruiting, talent management, and so on), and the entire life cycle of products from research (both internal and vendors) through the end of life for those materials. On one level, this just seems to be more functions, more enrichment, more inclusion, but each of these functional areas has process components that are part of an end-to-end business process. And now, these functional areas had to either be managed within the suite or modified such that all interactions with the back-office integration engine were consistent with process decisions that had been made in the initial implementation. Although on a business level, this was a good thing, on another level, it plunged companies back into the need to manage design, implementation, and change management within the organization, but now more broadly defined.

Just as in the introduction of R/3, the former name of the main ERP software produced by SAP AG, the opportunity arose for someone to step up to lead the process of designing and introducing change to the organization, not only at the worker level, but also with senior executives. Businesses were interested in adopting those parts of the new systems that could address what they had identified as problems with existing processes. They did not, however, understand the restrictions placed on the design teams to make the data and transactions consistent with organizational and master data models already adopted in the core software. In most cases, the IT department continued to present technology solutions to business problems, without having sufficient knowledge of, or respect from, the business. The business, however, continued to look to IT to deliver its new system to resolve issues and generally failed to comprehend challenges presented by the integration of the business suite with the ERP platform.

The technical capabilities being developed created great opportunity. However, they also widened the gap between business and IT in understanding how to get these applications deployed to effectively produce business benefits. Another opportunity was lost.

GETTING INFORMATION AND ANALYSIS OUT OF THE DATA OCEAN (1997–2007)

At the same time, more attention was being paid to enriching the ability of management to get better and cleaner access to analytics and reports. Data warehouses with more advanced analytical tools were developed, both by ERP vendors and by other competitors, and business content was added to enhance analytics and presentation layers. While data warehousing was a growth area by itself, the development of this tool in the early days was viewed by business mostly as a better way to generate the same types of reporting it had used for decades, and the capability to include analytics was poorly understood but was growing.

Why, then, is this important? Essentially, it turned around the design algorithm for reporting systems and provided the opportunity to gain more control over the ultimate outcome of the back-office transaction engine. Now, it was not only possible but should have been required that before designing and implementing ERP, management should be challenged to provide an outline of the information it needed to see as it decided how to operate the business. Most early reporting systems started with what was there, selected the data, organized it, and compiled the report.[3] User organizations would then find the reports to be lacking and ask for additional information, which could be added if it existed in the application or added to the system over time, if not. There was little to be gained by thinking about the business from an analytical perspective and then designing information back into the programs. This changed with the addition of data warehouses tied to the ERP packages, which could handle large amounts of data and, through cubes and queries, could produce a much larger assortment of views and analytics. Plus, it required businesses to define what data and reports would be important to their decision making.

Unfortunately, this type of thinking was rare. Management was accustomed to simply getting reports produced by the IT group from data that just existed, and Business Warehouse (BW) was seen as another "cool tool" that could be used to produce reports. Because IT continued to be viewed as technology, not as a business partner, dissatisfaction continued from the business community, with myriad requests for changes to the reports available to managers. The opportunity to present this developing capability as a business opportunity and to lead business executives in the design of new business analytics evolved sparingly and slowly.[4]

CORPORATE REPORTING AND DASHBOARDS (2007–TODAY)

Moving forward to the late 2000s, a solid back-office engine was installed, along with rich front-office functionality to connect the business with business partners, and a reasonably qualified reporting platform that could be modified and used flexibly was in place. It was a good time to address the issue of what a business should want to know, in order to both achieve strategic objectives and satisfy the need for tactical business improvements.

With end-to-end and wall-to-wall solutions now available, the time had come to focus business leaders on defining what was really needed in order to accurately see the condition of their business and to produce analytics to provide insight into where they should evolve strategically. This still applied both to strategic analysis (market segmentation) and to tactical planning (supply chain planning or productivity improvements). In order to get more structure and to enrich the business content of the analytical engine, ERP vendors acquired more capable and extensive reporting engines into a management front end that leaders can use to improve both visibility and timeliness of information. Although this goes a long way to provide packaged solutions based on proven business processes, it still does not provide business leaders with cut-and-paste solutions, but it offers a rich set of tools that can be used to implement a management approach once the direction is determined.

The obvious opportunity here was for IT to become a key business partner with operational leaders of the business, working through the design process. This required a determination of whether the data collected by the SAP platforms was sufficient to support the needs of the new solutions that they were recommending and to figure out how to get the data that didn't exist. This evolving role, more than ever, did and still does depend on the IT organization being a business partner and on internal business management consultancy to support functional business leaders.

One should note that throughout this view of the history of the software from a business perspective, IT's role has been emphasized, and IT's role was to maintain deep and broad technical knowledge of the system, the capabilities, and expansion in the richness of functionality. IT also needed to stay current with tools such as mobility solutions, portals, or graphic user-interface improvements and how these technologies have developed to further productivity improvements for workers. However, the real opportunity is for IT to become a business partner by expanding its view to that of advising business leaders of opportunities to use the technologies to produce measurable Return on Investment. Although mobility solutions, for example, are really cool and workers can gain access to certain functions on iPhones, iPads, and other devices, the ability to calculate the costs, work with business leaders to figure out how they can be applied, calculate the Return on Investment, and then work together to ensure that the benefits are realized is the real value that the IT business consultancy can contribute.

This is a different role for IT, and while IT workers and leaders still need to depend on their technical training, the real value to business is no longer just about technical solutions and project management; it requires an understanding of how these tools can be applied to produce tangible and measurable business benefits.

THE ERA OF GOVERNANCE: IMPLICATIONS FOR THE FUTURE

In examining today's environment, it is easy to get carried away with the technology advances. There is still a business to be led and business leaders continue to need advice from the IT function on how to effectively use technology to create business value and to measure Return on Investment. Much of what is coming today is focused on delivery, flexibility, and speed, which can offer significant advantages, but the business cases for near-term Return on Investment have often not been determined. Examples include:

1. **Cloud**. Perhaps not today but in the near future, the ability to deliver all of these applications over the Web will become a serious option for consideration. This is both from a cost and an architecture standpoint as applications become more mobile.
2. **Mobility**. With the advent of "smart" everything, opportunities to use the new technologies (iPhones, iPads, and so on) may allow for a more effective and efficient flow of work through the enterprise. The ability to provide everything from procurement release strategies to HR job-posting approvals over smartphones, so that approving managers are no longer tied to laptops or tedious surrogate assignments, may be effective in automating processes.

3. **In Memory Computing**. The continued dramatic reduction in the cost of memory now makes it reasonable to keep much more information accessible from primary transaction platforms and could ultimately require rethinking the entire architecture of business intelligence tools, but not yet.

These advances are all really cool and exciting and provide great speculation, on the part of both IT leaders and vendors about future potential. However, this, while important, may not be where the greatest opportunity resides for immediate business benefits.

An appropriate role for leaders today is to use this new capability for corporate financial governance—generally, and sometimes too narrowly, defined as Sarbanes-Oxley, IFRS, and other financial regulatory standards that must be met. The ability to use these systems to develop approaches to governance and risk management is expanding rapidly, both through vendor-supplied functionality and through the ability to construct collection and reporting tools that allow for closer monitoring of operations.

One should think beyond just another "collect, analyze, and report" task for a minute. While it is true that the financial function is primarily responsible for these tasks, the ability to use the processes that are instrumental in this analysis goes well beyond what is taught in accounting schools. It takes knowledge of regulatory standards and, as described in the last two sections, knowledge of the data that are available through design of the transaction system, knowledge of the business processes that are created by and enabled by the software configuration, and the ways in which these can be reconfigured to achieve the desired business process. Programs created to evaluate compliance with regulations in addition can be a good test of the integrity of the system. IT can take the view that establishing the use of this and similar programs can act as quality control over the system and, in doing so, can point out areas where integrity and accuracy can be enhanced. The whole subject of enterprise risk management seeks to evaluate risk well beyond just regulatory compliance, even to the point where corporate board members can exercise their responsibility to ensure that the enterprise acts to meet the needs of shareholders, employees, and customers.

 ## SUMMARY

This chapter outlines how the role of IT has needed to evolve during the previous decades from one of technical resources—mostly, programmers supporting one business function—to one of internal business consultants helping functional business leaders evaluate business objectives, design applications strategies to implement these decisions, and work with the data being gathered to ensure that proper analytics and controls are available to the leadership team. In the gulf between functional business leaders and IT leaders, the distribution of responsibilities needs to be reevaluated and better understood. Today, traditional functional leaders are on one end (traditional in both role and education) and technology workers are on the other end. In between, IT applications are now pervasive and define business processes, as well as to enable the delivery of business results. It is this space in between that has not been effectively managed, and this lack of management results in much of the "failure" of the applications to live up to expectations.

This book provides a road map for business leaders to use the ERP applications to achieve business benefits that have been promised but are difficult to realize. It will, however, require a different way of looking at business fundamentals and then of viewing them through the lens of the applications that defines and institutionalizes the business design. This chapter shows how business leadership roles could have evolved during the years that the new applications platforms were being built and implemented. In doing so, it also shows where the path to recovering the value left behind leads. The rest of this book looks at our way of viewing and analyzing some business fundamentals that need to change and providing a governance program to oversee the changes that are necessary—all toward the end of achieving the Return on Investment that is possible.

 NOTES

1. Michael Hammer and James Champy, *Re-engineering the Corporation: A Manifesto for Business Revolution* (New York: Harper Business Essentials, 1993).
2. Michael Doane, "Configure It Out: Why Business Should Own SAP Configuration," 2010. http://sapsearchlight.blogspot.com/2010/12/configure-it-out-why-business-should.html.
3. James Orlicky, *Material Requirements Planning: The New Way of Life in Production and Inventory Management* (New York: McGraw-Hill, 1975).
4. Oliver Wight, *Manufacturing Resource Planning: MRP II, Unlocking America's Productivity Potential* (Essex Junction, VT: Oliver Wight Limited Publications: 1981).

PART TWO

Contextual Analysis

P ART II DEALS with five aspects of operating businesses and proposes different approaches to understanding, analyzing, and designing transformation programs to achieve significant Return on Investment. The five analyses are used in Part III to construct a program governance approach to lead the organization through the change process and ensure that the intended benefits are achieved.

- Chapter 4, "Return on Investment—Developing the Business Case": This chapter presents unachieved Return on Investment as an undefined asset of the business. It then describes methods to identify, quantify, and organize the Return on Investment potential to pay for ERP programs.
- Chapter 5, "Business Process Analysis": This chapter discusses the relationship between business process management disciplines and the best business practices recommended in ERP applications. It further describes how to combine these relationships to create an optimal business process and recover Return on Investment.
- Chapter 6, "Business Culture, Politics, and Organization": This chapter discusses the roles that culture, politics, and organizational structure play in enabling or preventing changes to achieve Return on Investment. It presents

the case for understanding these interactions and learning how to work with these interactions to achieve intended benefits.

- Chapter 7, "IT Strategy Review": This chapter discusses how the way in which IT strategy is developed and implemented can have either positive or negative effects on the ability to achieve the planned Return on Investment.

- Chapter 8, "Workforce Education and Readiness": This chapter goes beyond simple project training and discusses how collective workforce knowledge can lead to more effective use of ERP applications and acceptance of changes that produce Return on Investment.

CHAPTER FOUR

Return on Investment—Developing the Business Case

"If a company is looking only at how much IT costs, that figure will always look too high. So a cornerstone of Mott's philosophy is to put a measurable value on the work the IT organization does—what he calls the 'revenue of IT.' That data represents all the benefits, both hard dollar and intangibles, that a project delivers in the 12 months following full implementation.

"Said Mott in 2008: 'Every business has revenue, but IT typically doesn't . . . because we don't have the discipline to capture the benefit of projects in a way that we can show the CEO or executive committee and have numbers that are real.'"

—Excerpt from "10 Lessons in IT Strategy from Ex-HP CIO Randy Mott," Information Week

INTRODUCTION

Return on Investment justification is a standard part of business planning. If a business is deciding to build a new manufacturing plant, it is necessary to determine whether it makes financial sense to invest in this project. The calculation of the profit that the new facility will provide is compared to the cost to design and build it. The expectation is that once the business case is developed and approved and the project completed, the business will be held responsible to produce the forecast results. This chapter deals with the development and incorporation of an effective Return on Investment case for investments in new information technology where business issues have frequently prevented this from being used effectively. Although there may well be some aspects of ERP systems that enable other processes and don't produce results, in and of themselves, there are very few, and the vast majority should be launched only when it is clear that they will provide a tangible, measurable, believable, and desirable financial benefit to the business. Unfortunately, a large number of IT applications programs have not had specific Return on Investment targets, or the cases are so poorly prepared and executed that measurement becomes impossible and the programs are allowed to devolve into a "cost of doing business" approach. An effective Return on Investment business case is essential to enabling any organization to achieve planned benefits from new functionality. Part III will offer a program that merges all of the components from this section into a program where the relationships among the business components are merged into a continuous improvement program.

In developing a Return on Investment case for an organization, it is necessary to advocate for a different approach. Typically the scope and intent of a program is developed first and then planners set out to find justification for the investment. Turning this sequence around, we can identify opportunities for potential business improvements before the actual programs are developed. Potential Return on Investment should be seen as an undisclosed asset of the business—profitability that is logically possible, if you can figure out how to get it.

The phrase "return on investment" has been used so often that it has nearly become a joke in some circles. For years, large capital investments were always justified based on a business model that demonstrated the length of time that it would take to make enough profit to repay the company for the investment. This was coauthor Art Worster's experience with yearly $20M expansions during the 1970s, was the case for two new plant facilities designed and built in the 1980s, and should be the case for any of today's programs, including ERP implementations. After all, with very few exceptions, if the investment won't eventually pay for itself, what earthly reason would there be for doing it?

Although this investment analysis case has been carried over onto IT projects, the business case is rarely completed to any believable degree. The source of the Return on Investment is often left ill-defined, and the interaction between the new program and other activities is rarely defined. The base case is typically either not developed or developed but never accepted by business leaders. The most unbelievable factor in all of this is that failure is not only tolerated, but often anticipated, even before the program begins. The lack of understanding is rampant, regarding how to go through the process of developing and executing an IT project, with the expectation of successfully producing the Return on Investment from the business case. For this reason, many companies have just given up and anticipate that all IT applications projects are going to cost more than budgeted, take longer than planned, produce fewer tangible results than predicted, and often fail altogether. The phrase "cost of doing business" is typically used to describe this. Then various methods are used to try to keep the overruns within guidelines, formal or informal. Fundamentally, this is a unreliable and uncontrollable way to run any kind of business. Instead, we will take another approach to getting control and will focus on providing business value to the enterprise.

Before we do that, however, let's take a moment to consider exactly what Return on Investment cases are. There are a number of different financial models for calculating Return on Investment, and we are not going to elaborate on them here. For our purposes, let's just consider that the model will define all of the costs and all of the benefits and will include methods for calculating net present value to take into account future devaluations of returns such as inflation. There is still a significant lack of understanding of some Return on Investment calculations. Here are a couple of examples, one from the perspective of cost reduction and the other from the perspective of increased revenue based on increased sales.

EXAMPLE 1: COST REDUCTION

In many cost-reduction programs, inventory elimination (of all types) will be a significant component of anticipated benefits. In order to properly estimate the overall returns on these reductions, there are many components that have to be taken into consideration, some reduced costs and some increased costs in the near term, but all must be considered. What is included is a product of what type of inventory you are eliminating. For example, if you are reducing warehouse stores (spare parts for machinery that are stocked for repair orders), then you may be eliminating obsolete or excess inventory. In either case, you must calculate the book value of the inventory as costs and offset this with the benefits that you accrue, which may include reduced notional interest on the working capital, decreased storage costs by freeing up space for other needed parts or for other uses, and so on. Often, however, it can become much more complex.

Some years ago, we had a large amount of excess finished goods inventory that was to be reduced through modifications in the way inventory was ordered, the way production campaigns were planned, and the amount of safety stock. The division staff had approved the reduction in inventory because the remaining inventory would be better targeted to demand and would also improve customer service simultaneously. Inventory restocking orders for the new targets were calculated and entered, manufacturing runs planned and executed, and the inventory target was met. During the ensuing staff meeting, however, other effects (none of which were included in the Return on Investment calculation that the IT expenditures were based on) of the inventory reduction became evident. If you don't increase sales, you have to reduce production in order to decrease inventory (seems pretty intuitive); however, projected profit for the month was based on a planned amount of production and manufacturing overhead, as well as plant overhead, and was a part of the total cost basis of the financial planning model. With severely reduced production for several months, the result was a manufacturing volume variance-to-budget, meaning that profitability decreased during that period, becoming an unpredicted surprise to the staff. One can argue that it should not have been a surprise; however, many components of the Return on Investment calculation may not be intuitive to all leaders and should be included at the start of the program.

When you calculate Return on Investment, you must take into account all costs and benefits, which include the following:

- Increased cash flow as working capital is converted to cash.
- Lower profits while inventory is reduced due to slower production.
- Overhead absorption.
- Less working capital; therefore reduced notional interest (a positive contribution).

- Decreased ancillary benefits such as reduced shrinkage, handling, space consumption, and so on.

Once all of these costs and benefits are identified and predicted, they have to be analyzed by financial analytics to demonstrate the overall Return on Investment for the program. In our case, despite the unpredicted negative variance that had to be explained to the business group, the actual benefits that accrued from the inventory reduction program would have justified the program anyway. Yet this is not always the case and is one of the reasons why leaders frequently distrust Return on Investment cases.

EXAMPLE 2: GREATER MANUFACTURING CAPACITY LEADING TO INCREASED SALES

In this example, manufacturing capacity was not sufficient to keep up with demand, mostly due to issues with logistics and manufacturing planning. Sales were on allocation, so demand already existed to absorb additional production capacity. In this case, through re-implementing in-plant logistics movements among receiving, intermediate storage, raw material warehouse, and the manufacturing floor, plant management was able to ensure that it always knew what material was available, where it was, and how to move the material to the reactor vessels at the time that it was needed. This reduced downtime spent waiting for materials or for unplanned change-overs (which caused waste and lost time) allowed more time for the production of sales materials. Because the overhead of the division had already been absorbed by the existing production and was operating profitably, the additional production using the same resources meant that gross margins were the same as net margins and had a disproportionately high positive impact on profitability. This is the phenomena where the only incremental costs were the variable costs of production, such as raw materials, energy, and others. How this works and is calculated, however, depends on where the plant is on the manufacturing capacity scale. The point here is that there is a calculable positive impact on the sales that results from improved manufacturing efficiency, which is also a Return on Investment. Often, in fact, this impact may have fewer short-term negative costs associated with it, and it can be a dramatic contributor to justifying manufacturing investments.

In this case, contributions to profitability for Return on Investment calculations were based on the fully burdened cost of manufacturing, which reduced the real positive impact of the investment. Because the business case was not compelling with this calculation method, the project was approved as a "cost of doing business," and the surprises that occurred were all positive. Often, however, this may not be the case, and failure to include all negative and positive benefits into the calculation may skew the analysis and result in decisions that delay or derail programs that can provide positive benefits to the business.

PROVIDING BUSINESS VALUE TO AN ENTERPRISE

The steps to providing business value to an enterprise include the following:

1. Identify improvement opportunities.
2. Identify current Return on Investment projects/programs.
3. Identify ownership issues.
4. Identify probable causes.
5. Design new business processes.
6. Identify areas of conflict between functional areas.
7. Build a believable return on investment case.
8. Establish a governance process at the executive level.

Identify Improvement Opportunities

Identifying improvement opportunities were discussed briefly in Chapter 2. The point is that in virtually every organization, the areas in which organizations know they have an opportunity for improvement are well known. In many cases, these opportunities may not be articulated for political reasons, but they are known. In others, the opportunities are articulated incessantly. Yet these opportunities are never discussed with the intent to build programs for which leaders will be held accountable.

There are many reasons for this that have evolved over the years, and the results are predictable. There is a principle in the industrial safety field that states: workers will always live up to minimum expectations, which means, for example, if the penalty for not wearing safety glasses is to be told to put them on, then the expectation is not that workers will wear them, but that they will put them on every time they are told. The same principle applies to developing, committing to, and delivering Return on Investment cases. Over the years, we have become accustomed to failures for many reasons.

- The business case is not believable.
- The scope is not properly defined, and changes are not managed properly.
- Time lines are not committed to on a critical path.
- Project management is weak and/or not empowered.

And many more. Here are some additional examples:

- Let's say you are in a commodity business, and your total inventory turns (that is, the number of times inventory turns over in a year—typically, 8 to 12 in a commodity business) are 5, and you know your competition's turnover is much higher, yet you may not know why your business is experiencing 5, but you surely know that it needs to improve.
- If you are a make-to-stock business, and your days of back orders (total back orders divided by average daily sales) are 30 (or some similar number), you may not know why you have this disconnect between manufacturing and sales, but you surely know that it exists.
- If reporting on your monthly financial closing process is barely done before the next month is ready to close, you may not know why it is so difficult, but you surely know that there are problems.

And the list goes on.

At the very least, you only have to look at the objectives for the top several levels of management to get a pretty complete starting list. Why, for example, would a department manager have an objective to reduce headcount in his or her department by increasing productivity, if leadership did not know or at least suspect that headcount was either too high or higher than could be achieved by reducing redundancy, eliminating errors, creating more accurate reporting, and improving many more practices?

In most organizations, if you collected the objectives for the top several levels of management, collated, and analyzed them, at least two things would become clear.

1. First, the obvious conclusion would be that the organization is not at a loss for ideas regarding how to continuously improve performance.
2. Second, there are objectives within the organization that are in conflict, often mutually impossible, and when incentive programs are created to boost success on these objectives, the organization has what is referred to as "destructive incentives." Sometimes these destructive incentives

appear to be in conflict and are not. For the most part, however, they are in conflict, without resolution, and many needed improvement opportunities are lost. These conflicts and resolutions will be addressed in Chapter 11.

In another example, let's take an organization with three times the healthy amount of total inventory, and, at the same time, the organization is experiencing extremely high levels of back orders and issues around product quality and delivery timing. Sales, in this case, have an incentive to reduce back orders, distribution has an incentive to improve delivery time performance, and manufacturing has an incentive to reduce inventory. The resolution may come in IT applications that tie the three together into a cross-functional business process. Yet in order to get the design and implementation done, adjustments have to be made for all three areas. If there is not a process that aligns the objectives of the three organizations and provides a method for arriving at a single integrated process design, it will make the process much more difficult and could easily derail it entirely. The Return on Investment potential, however, is real and needs to be seen as an asset waiting to be discovered and recovered. Using this asset approach to undisclosed returns creates organizational focus on recovery and improved performance.

Other methods similar to this can be used to identify areas where there are definable targets for improvement. Just walking, either literally, in the case of manufacturing, or figuratively, in the case of sales and markets, through the business slowly and thoughtfully, you can find logical "holes" where these improvement opportunities lie. This is as simple as the story of the "gold nuggets" from Chapter 1 or may be as obscure as a recent reduction in sales in one region, but they are there if expert leaders will only stop, look, and observe (STOP, the Stop to Observe Program). By any method, this part of the analysis is designed to list all areas where an organization imagines there can be improvements, regardless of whether the organization may have any idea how to achieve the changes or what the potential for improvement may be. Although pain may be caused by any number of events, including some self-inflicted, it is usually a good place to start to look and analyze.

As a word of caution, many organizations seem to go out of their way to enlist workers in this cause by talking about the increase in productivity that could result, which easily translates into lost jobs—not exactly an incentive for workers to be forthcoming. If productivity and jobs really are the final objectives, this may be unavoidable. Frequently, however, the major gains are in reduction of inventory, improvement of manufacturing cycle times, better performance in the market, and others. As much as you can focus on those objectives, which usually are worth much more, the easier it is to enlist employees in helping with this identification process. This might be as simple as establishing cross-training programs to retrain workers or to institute workforce reduction through turnover, rather than layoffs. Some years ago, an organization we worked with achieved a $19M turnaround in inventory reductions, manufacturing utilization improvements, and increased sales. On top of this, it had the potential to also eliminate six jobs in manufacturing. Fortunately, the organization committed to reduction through attrition, which created a positive environment for achieving the much larger benefits that were attainable. Regardless of the methods used, the process must be addressed.

Identify Current Return on Investment Projects/Programs

Once these opportunities are identified, it is necessary to list all current work or projects that are justified by a Return on Investment, because these need to be incorporated into the new program. There can only be one program, and all facets need to be aligned with one set of intended results, with the exception of current programs where the Return on Investment is completely outside of the areas identified for new programs. The point is, when you have programs where funding was granted based on a commitment to deliver results, and now you want to create another program and use the same improvement targets, either the organization will allow it, which fosters conflict over who claims the improved results, or the organization will be reluctant to approve the new program, except when it is based on entirely new results, despite the fact that the results can be achieved only by combining the two work streams.

In a fully integrated enterprise, there can be only one comprehensive improvement program that defines all intended returns. This does not mean that the current programs cannot be allotted part of the returns to justify continuing with them. One must keep in mind that the inherent conflict between programs must be resolved during the planning stages. When current Return on Investment–based projects are not in conflict with the ERP programs, the projects should be allowed to continue. However, the projects should be catalogued under this analysis for a couple of reasons, including the following:

1. When IT applications are changed and new business processes implemented, there are often impacts well beyond the initial obvious changes

(law of unintended consequences). These can often create conflict with current ongoing programs, regardless of whether this conflict is obvious at the outset.
2. It may well be that the current improvements are based on what might be possible with the current systems. It may, however, also be true that more dramatic changes with the new system can not only achieve the benefits from the current program but can bring about far more benefits when done together.

The largest detractor found from listing and incorporating these is that IT projects tend to be too lengthy to start with, are prone to miss delivery dates, and rarely gain the benefits advertised. Thus, history is not your friend. Yet as part of developing this program, the organization must revise past perceptions and change expectations. As we construct our new continuous improvement process, we will flatten the investment curve, focus on shorter projects, and insist that these improved processes successfully deliver the intended results, as covered in Part III of this book.

Identify Ownership Issues

Some years ago, one of this book's coauthors experienced what is known as a "360 degree assessment" of how he was viewed by the organization. In that assessment, a peer said, "If there is a flat tire, he will change it, regardless of whose car it is on." Although he took this as a compliment, it was clearly not meant as such. This demonstrates the necessity to figure out who in the organization "owns" each piece, who believes that he or she does, and who used to but no longer does and is still emotionally attached to the design. In this case, the departments in question were Customer Service and Sales Administration, both of which reported to Shared Services; however, the sales organization really believed that how those departments operated was their responsibility. In addition, there were people in the sales organization who had designed the original process, were no longer responsible for it, and were sensitive to the perception that the design was a problem. In fact, the problems that were hampering the organization were not with the design or the people responsible for it but were with management decisions on how some of the rules were to be implemented.

Failure on our part to fully investigate who in the organization had "pride of authorship" and to include them in the redesign process, such that they fully understood the reasons for the changes and that these were not precipitated by something that had been done wrong in the past, created unnecessary resistance to change. The view that their input and historical value were not appreciated was the outcome of this oversight. In nearly every design process, you will encounter these or similar issues, and they can be detected and dealt with early by paying attention to them in the design process.

Failure to recognize these issues and sensitivities could well have derailed some of our programs, if it were not for the fact that over time we replaced all of the IT business applications that operated in those departments and, in so doing, resolved the issues and institutionalized the changes. The resentment, however, did not go away with the success of the program and the elimination of unnecessary costs. In most organizations, the ability to design and enact cross-functional changes of this type is limited at best. It is, therefore, necessary to establish a process of requiring discussion of the interaction between departments and ultimately to settle on an acceptable resolution that is consistent with achieving the committed Return on Investment. Failure to include ownership issues in this discussion may well derail a well-conceived and well-executed project.

Identify Probable Causes

Because we now have an understanding of ownership issues, areas of opportunity, and a list of existing Return on Investment–based projects, it is time to have a process discussion around what probable causes can be identified. Hopefully, the analysis group has created along the way the potential for collaborative discussions between departments so that this can proceed easily. If not, this discussion can be a critical point in the investigative process, and it would be difficult to spend too much time on gaining understanding, agreements, and commitments that will be needed later. We learned from Dr. Deming that issues are rarely caused by "bad people" but are instead the result of good people being restrained or subverted by bad business processes. Because many workers, however, tend to identify with their jobs and how they are performed, this part of the analysis can be tricky. Nevertheless, it is often people working in the process who really know what is wrong, have probably talked about it for a long time, may have given up long ago, and, with care, can be enlisted in the process as supporters of changes. A little time spent now can save a lot of time later.

In the step to analyze and redesign business processes, tools will be selected to facilitate this. Even here, however, for complex issues that are identified, it may be useful to employ methods to identify the most probable causes of the problem. In complex discussions, tools such as Failure Mode and Effect Analysis or Fault Tree Analysis may be useful. Although these are tools more typically used in process design in the chemical industry or in safety reviews for engineering programs, they may also be useful during this phase. Both of them, as well as others, simply take the approach of breaking down issues along logical relationships and analyzing possible errors and their effects.

Often the causes can also be far from where the symptoms occur. Some years ago, an issue was encountered when a plant was not able to ship product that was sitting on the shipping department floor because the ERP application did not know that the lot number existed. On investigation, it turned out that the production department could not confirm the final step on the production order (which would have created the finished goods inventory lot number and consumed raw material inventory) because the ERP application showed that the raw material inventory did not exist. Further investigation found that the receivers for raw material inventory had not been entered as it was received (there was plenty of inventory, just not recognized by the ERP program) because the receiving department supervisor had been taken ill, and nobody else had been trained to enter receipts into the system. The point in telling this story is not one of business process design. It clearly demonstrates, however, that often a totally unsuspected event elsewhere in the business process causes the initial failure. It may well be that the people working on this analysis either cannot determine probable causes or may not have broad enough knowledge of the whole business process to establish where the improvement opportunities exist. In that case, just cataloguing the opportunity, the symptoms, and the costs can be kept as a placeholder for business process analysis and design teams. Every case will be different, but getting a handle on probable causes at this point is necessary.

Design New Business Processes

Using business process design programs of some sort helps identify failure points, faulty handoffs, and broken processes, within the larger cross-functional business process definitions. Here, broader business process definitions are necessary to ensure that the resolution of issues identified is consistent with the broader view of the business. However, it is often important to refine this to a more granular level, in order to make the relationships work. The actual redesign of business processes is covered in Chapter 5. Yet because this analysis has determined many of the failure points in the organization, it is a valuable discussion to be had during the discovery of Return on Investment potential.

For example, finished goods inventory may depend highly on sales forecasting for average levels of stock. However, it is critical in a business that is heavily dependent on trade promotions to have an effective way to incorporate the results of a trade promotion into demand on a regional level and ways to know quickly whether the increased sales are temporary, based on the promotion, or are part of normal demand. Often this can be a case of increased sales during the promotion because customers are simply "buying ahead," which means decreased sales in the subsequent period. The relationship between regional distribution center inventories and forecasting and tracking of promotions is very detailed, quite localized, and necessary. Yet the relationship must also be considered in the broader order-to-cash cycle that includes financial planning, the rest of the supply chain, and manufacturing planning.

The design of these business processes will deal extensively with the handoff points, where the responsibility for one or more parts of the process may pass from one functional area to another. The perceptions of participants in this analysis can provide good input to process design teams that will consider all of the cross-functional failure points and eventually develop the new business processes. For example, if the ability to have correct inventory in the correct regional location in order to support a trade promotion is critical to the promotion, the correct inventory could result in $XX of increased sales with $YY of increased profit. Thus, identifying this as potential Return on Investment to the business process design group is important.

Identify Areas of Conflict between Functional Areas

To help the business design teams, analysis of opportunities will inevitably identify areas of actual or potential conflict between functions or even lines of business. As an example, if one functional department head will no longer be able to achieve an objective on which compensation or promotion could be based, that objective will have to be changed outside of the yearly management by objective (or similar) cycle and perhaps even incentive compensation programs revised mid-year. You cannot expect an executive to negatively affect his or her own career path by placing barriers in mid-cycle and have the changes embraced. We have found that management teams that do analyses such as this tend to shy away from identifying areas of conflict. Conversely, we have also found that identifying these areas objectively so that they can be dealt with or incorporated into either design or change processes can provide program managers with an early look into potential problems and/or resolutions. A full analysis of corporate culture at executive levels, as well as an understanding of the political structure of the leadership organization, will be fully discussed in Chapter 6, but since many contentious issues are going to be identified during the investigation of Return on Investment potential, these issues need to be collected so that they can be part of the design process discussed in Chapter 9.

One additional point worth mentioning here and discussed in much more detail later is that whenever we refer to cultural and political issues that must be identified, we are talking about an objective appraisal of these characteristics of all organizations. The fact is that any organization of two or more people will have both a culture and a political structure. There may, in fact, be such a thing as "bad politics" or the Machiavellian idea. For our purposes, however, we will describe what these structures are and how they affect the ability of an organization to achieve the business benefits it seeks, and we will stay away as much as possible from characterizations of them. This also, incidentally, applies to organizational concepts. All enterprises have an organization that defines them, so blaming things on the organization, just as blaming the culture or the politics, may feel good and be easy but does nothing to help us figure out how to address it or use it to achieve intended results. It is not having an organizational concept that is important; it is in knowing how to use or change the organization to be one that can be employed to produce intended business benefits that brings value. Again, this will be discussed in Chapter 6 and will also play an important role in the following discussion.

Build a Believable Return on Investment Case

With a clear view of the "as is" financial picture and with a projection of what potential exists, you can construct a Return on Investment case, at least in macro terms. In a typical organization, this may have been estimated at the start of the process—identifying improvement opportunities. Now that you have completed the intervening steps, you can put some hard numbers both to the cost of developing new processes and to the value you estimate can be created, either in reduced costs or increased revenues. Yet due to past experiences, many organizations lose confidence in the process at this point. This is typical because too many programs have been built on the same savings, nobody ever believed the starting-point model, and programs competed for resources (or, in some cases, were even at odds with one another).

Also, past experience has created a risk avoidance mentality in many leadership teams, where they still "intend" to achieve the return on investment but are reluctant to put these objectives into clear-cut, measurable goals that they will be held accountable to achieve. As with everything else in business, clear objectives, clear measurements, and clear accountability are needed to keep programs on track and achieve potential benefits.

A business group of a large global organization was losing nearly 10 percent based on revenue on $1.3B in sales. Through reengineering studies, the study groups identified more than $100M in potential savings that could be realized through implementation of the reengineered business processes. The implementation, however, would have to include the replacement of the legacy IT systems with an integrated ERP set of applications. Based on very detailed studies and plans, the savings were virtually unarguable, and certainly the need was painfully obvious. For many of the reasons covered in this chapter—bad historical experience, ownership issues between divisions, competing programs based on Return on Investment, and others—the operating council was unable to commit to achieving the targets as justification for the program, which was to cost nearly $50M and was still a six-month payback (normally a slam dunk for approval).

Eventually, a decision to proceed cautiously into the planning phase was made, but to justify the work as a "cost of doing business" was certainly nothing to inspire anyone to undergo potentially painful changes. You have only to read the literature about not achieving business benefits to recognize that this is a "good news vs. bad news" scenario, in many cases. The bad news is that Return on Investment was not achieved as planned; the good news is that it is still there to be taken, if the organization can refocus on the issues and conflicts that resulted in failure.

Establish a Governance Process at the Executive Level

Leadership at this point must take over and lead the process. The approach expressed in this book to create Return on Investment programs is designed to deal with these issues. The executive team must get to the point where it believes the base case, the estimates of improvements, and the approach being taken. All too often, this is the point where executives get cold feet, realizing that their careers, compensation, and personal reputation are going to be at stake. They further realize that their success will be dependent on not only their individual efforts but also the team efforts shared with others whom they may have traditionally been at odds with.

Before allowing these fears to sabotage the effort, which is typical of what happens today, each member of the leadership team needs to become totally committed to a governance process. This governance process will be a key to the success of the project, as well as a key to the success of individuals who will have the responsibility to work through these issues with the team. As difficult as this may be in a highly competitive political and cultural environment, it is at this juncture that the team must confront the realization that only a process like this will ultimately lead to the group's success, which is required or desired.

Andrew Spanyi, in his book titled *Business Process Management Is a Team Sport*, defines how analyzing business processes, identifying weaknesses and failure points, designing new processes, and implementing these processes are a collaborative effort among all of the functional leaders and workers.[1] Spanyi is certainly right in this case. It is a governance process such as one that will be described in Chapter 10, as well as detailed preparation and execution that allow for success to occur. This success will start with the creation of a compelling financial case that is believable and executable, along with a continuous governance process that will become part of the new culture of the enterprise.

 SUMMARY

Now, it's time to establish a governance process at the executive level that will manage the information gathered and the knowledge gained, which will be covered in Part III. You now have a believable and executable Return on Investment case built that has the buy-in of all of the key business executives. In Part III, we propose a program governance structure that will take the output from this chapter and the next four in Part II and merge these together into a program to work with business leaders to ensure that the anticipated benefits are achieved. The key to managing business transformation is a process to incorporate change itself as a managed process in long-term business planning. Many organizations that have experienced failure to achieve the benefits that they know are available have been unable to establish a clear and sustainable vision of what can be achieved. The next four chapters discuss other failure points along this path, but none are any more important than the process of establishing where current failure points are and what the potential is for creating future value.

As an organization looks at the money it has to invest in improvement or expansion programs, unrealized Return on Investment should be viewed as money to be spent if it can meet the investment guidelines established by the business. Assuming that the business has the ability to generate the capital, what business would not take on a program that would pay for itself in a year and bank every subsequent year of reduced costs or increased revenue and the profitability improvements that come with it?

 NOTE

1. Andrew Spanyi, *Business Process Management Is a Team Sport* (Tampa: Anclote Press, 2003).

CHAPTER FIVE

Business Process Analysis

"The business process you use today has been perfectly designed to produce today's business results."

—A paraphrase of many authors

 ## INTRODUCTION

Although often not recognized as such, the quote above is clearly a tautology if you accept the premise that business results don't just occur, but instead occur because of the way a business operates, which is defined by the business processes they employ. To say it another way, all organizations employ a set of business applications that allows them to conduct business in a manner they have chosen, either by detailed design or by default. How these applications are constructed and executed will ultimately determine how the business performs.

Without changing the functionality of IT applications that an enterprise operates on, it is impossible to change the business processes that enable the corporation or to alter results in any sustainable fashion. This set of applications is referred to as the enterprise applications platform, whether it is a modern ERP system such as SAP, Oracle, and others, or it is a combination of proprietary functional applications cobbled together to support the business. How these systems are designed and implemented is knowledge that is critical to the performance of any business. In order to have an organization perform effectively, this must be understood to appropriate degrees at all levels and across all functions of the organization.[1]

There is more to this than simply education of the workforce, from executive leadership to workers in the organization. This book focuses on ERP systems specifically due to their broad acceptance, and because they provide real-time integration of all back-office functions that are already complete in the software. When successfully implemented, ERP systems have necessitated addressing logical design issues between departments. The only real difference between ERP systems and other enterprise applications platforms is in the timing of transactional impacts and the need to condition these impacts through interfaces, perhaps a necessity, but often not a positive design. The point is that it is perfectly possible to create and operate on proprietary applications developed for a specific company and to manage the design, development, implementation, and operation of that enterprise application platform properly to support the business. It is, however, expensive to operate and support new business needs when that is not one of the core competencies of the company. In addition, few companies other than business applications developers have and are able to maintain the competence to continue development of these systems over the years during which the business will continue to evolve. This leads to the need to clearly delineate the approach a company will take to define, design, implement, and use its enterprise applications platform and, in most cases, select one of the leading packages on the market today. This selection, however, should just be the start of the business transformation.

 ## WHERE ARE WE HEADED?

As described in Chapter 3, the evolution of ERP platforms during the last two decades has dramatically increased the number of tools that are available to leadership groups to help define, support, and institutionalize changes to business processes and improve overall business performance. Also from Chapter 2, the amount of knowledge of business processes in general, cross-functional integration specifically, and the design approaches necessary to effectively deploy these systems have not kept up with the potential that they represent to achieve a return on investment for the business. This is never more obvious than when we come to business process analysis/design/reengineering. Management groups continue to ask questions such as

- Are we going to ERP or BOB? (best of breed)
- Will we implement ERP or SOA? (services oriented architecture)

These are not questions that add value to the discussion and generally reflect the attitude that these systems are all about IT, when ultimately they are all about business needs. The leadership of any organization must decide on a design for the enterprise applications platform that usually includes an ERP core but may also include some best of breed (BOB) systems. These will very likely all be tied together using services oriented architecture (SOA), whether that is in native integration tools (SAP Netweaver or Oracle Fusion) or is on a fully proprietary platform. Beyond that, these integration tools will continue to evolve during the next decades and may provide yet more and different approaches to the design of business applications. What won't change, however, is the fundamental logic that relates business functions to one another. People don't invent business logic; people simply invent ways to design business processes that use this logic to create repeatable and consistent tools to manage a business using this logic. As expressed earlier, ERP systems can illuminate these logical relationships and provide design teams with an opportunity to eliminate redundancy and misalignment between departments, thereby improving overall organizational efficiency and profitability. Design teams have to eliminate talk of competing packages and focus on the following principle:

> The goal of any organization in selecting IT applications must be to provide the most comprehensive set of business applications that will support fundamental business logic and enable designs to produce optimal business results.

This is the enterprise applications platform and will potentially include a competent back-office system that fully integrates core functions of the enterprise, including logistics, financial, and HR. Beyond that, the platform may also include technologies that allow a business to work closely with customers, suppliers, employees, products (research to obsolescence), and supply chains to create ecosystems to optimize the performance across the extended enterprise, as well as functional tools designed to resolve specific issues an enterprise may have. Finally, the enterprise applications platform will provide data management, analytics, reporting, mobility, and other technology tools that give the most effective support to the overall organization. Just to make this list complete, any platform (whether a commercial package or a proprietary design) will also come with all of the technology components that enable it to operate effectively. These technology platform components are the only part of this suite that have always been and will likely remain exclusively the responsibility of the IT function. The problem up to now has been that virtually all of the components listed have been seen as IT functions and not as business responsibilities.

Where these come from should, more likely, be the last question asked, not the first. As a corollary of this, we also need to clearly state how we will delineate business processes; choose the approach we will use to analyze, design, and change these processes; and, finally, determine the technology tools that we will use to define, implement, and manage this entire transformation. This chapter is a discussion specifically of the discipline of process design and how that relates to the enterprise applications platform, specifically ERP systems. The lack of discussion on one or more of these areas has led to a compartmentalization of thinking, with proponents of one approach or another competing on an "us or them" basis for selection. The answer, as with nearly everything else in life, is to get back to the basics of understanding how all of the interrelated parts actually connect with one another and how actions taken in one area have both intended and unintended consequences for many others. As stated previously, ERP is also a tool that illuminates logical relationships, makes more results predictable, and helps an organization beat the law of unintended consequences.

 ## BUSINESS PROCESS DESIGN

Business process and its relationship to ERP implementation, as well as to business process reengineering in general, have been an enigma for nearly two decades, as described in Chapter 3. We have vacillated back and forth between "pure" reengineering, where IT applications are not considered until the process is designed and, on the other end, the use of recommended business processes (or best business practices) defined by the applications vendors. Often too little attention is given to the fundamental understanding necessary to design an optimal solution. We tend to either defer to current processes or grasp onto new processes as magic bullets. Neither of these approaches works well.

What is required is fundamental knowledge of the relationship between business processes and business performance, as well as knowledge of potential solutions (business practices) in the selected IT application platforms. In an integrated ERP world, we simply don't have the ability to sort out issues in interface designs. As usual, this starts with business knowledge, which is not startling, in and of itself. When analyzed and laid out, however, the sorting out of issues in interface designs calls for a level of process thinking that may well be both startling and perhaps even threatening to many. A sad aspect of this process is that collectively in an organization, knowledge of these areas exists, but the cultural and political process may seriously hinder the ability to use it effectively. Four basic sets of knowledge for business process analysis and design that we need to start with are

1. Business knowledge at the process level, which today is typically at functional levels.
2. Knowledge of how current IT applications define those processes.
3. Knowledge of what native business processes exist in both the existing and the proposed IT applications.
4. Process thinking discipline, or seeing the connections and influences, not just the pieces.

A clear distinction must be understood between functional and process knowledge. We all have knowledge that we have developed or acquired through the assignments we have had during our careers and lives. This knowledge allows us to remember how to perform the tasks in our jobs, how to organize our lives and workplaces, and, basically, how to live and succeed from day to day. In many instances, this knowledge is factual, is accurate, and defines "things" as we see them or learn them but that can better be described as snapshots, rather than movies. There is certainly nothing wrong with that; it is the basic learning method that we use throughout our lives.

There is, however, another aspect of knowledge that we need to consider. As much as our world involves "things," it also involves the connections between things and the ways in which they interact and relate to how results change from this dynamic relationship. This is process thinking—understanding the relationships and interactions between "things" and how actions in one area can have both intended and unintended consequences in others. Process thinking is what is necessary to properly create effective business designs. As we lead our lives, we become better and better at seeing these relationships and acting in ways that avoid pain and create benefits. Often we continue to learn these relationships empirically—by error, by retrying and perhaps eventually achieving success. The problem is that if the learning process stops there, and everything has to be learned through mistakes, the time line for success and the costs quickly become excessive. An observation of one logical relationship frequently also applies to many others, if you are able to understand why some things work and others do not. The ability to use process analysis and apply it to business process design is the competency required for this to be successful, in business, as in life.

The challenge is that these interrelationships are logical connections between things that exist in the world and are not artificial creations. Learning them is more about being able to see them, rather than designing them, but the thought process that allows us to discover them is often overlooked. An example is driving an automobile. We have designed the systems that make an automobile go, stop, turn, and so on. We can understand the mechanics of the process and learn each piece from the accelerator through linkage to the throttle to the fuel control systems and ultimately to turning fuel into energy to make the vehicle go. Learning to drive, however, is not about learning each of the mechanical pieces that go into providing the power to the vehicle; it is about understanding the process that requires depressing your foot onto the accelerator. It is about learning how varying pressure on the accelerator causes different actions from the car. It is much the same in business. It is not about learning what inventory is, what orders are, what manufacturing demand is—it is about learning how each of these relate to the others and how actions on one of them has consequences for the others. The more of these consequences we learn and include in our designs, the fewer will end up being unanticipated.

 ## PROCESS UNDERSTANDING REVEALS COMPLEXITY

A corollary of the statement in the subhead above, when applied to a functionally organized business (nearly all are today), is that if process thinking evaluates the connections between "things," it is unlikely that all of the "things" will belong to the same owner. Thus, as functions in IT applications become integrated, as they do in ERP applications, these ownership issues will inevitably be across multiple departments, further complicating the process of defining and designing these processes.

The following is a basic example of this process. If your goal is to reduce finished goods inventory that belongs to distribution, and there appear to be issues with the sales forecast, which belongs to sales and marketing, we need to be sure that we put in place a process to effectively deal with these boundary issues. Another example is the case of vendor selection for materials. If the procurement function has initiated vendor certification programs as part of the incentive for vendors to participate in market share distribution, then typically an algorithm will be established determining whom the next order goes to. If manufacturing, for various quality or operability reasons, prefers to have material from one vendor, rather than another, the issue can put the two departments at odds with each other. In this case, it will likely also be part of the yearly objectives of procurement to institute vendor certification, while it will be an objective of manufacturing to decrease waste or increase output, again, potentially in conflict with each other. When designing a business process in an ERP platform, how this shared responsibility will work must be dealt with in the business process design phase, which is also why understanding how the culture dictates that these conflicts will be handled is critical to success, as we will discuss in Chapter 6.

 ## BUSINESS PROCESS MANAGEMENT

Business process management practitioners generally recommend to senior leaders the following steps to deal with the business process design approach:

- Define the 6 to 10 cross-functional business processes that describe your organization.
- Assign business process owners who will have oversight responsibility for their process.
- Identify approaches to understanding existing processes, focusing on problems, issues, and opportunities for improvements, particularly looking at those places where errors occur or where handoffs between departments are problematic or inefficiencies exist (a process of selecting analysis and design tools).
- Design process flows between transactions or events that address these issues.

One of the problems encountered with the approach of many business process management practitioners today is that they have been stuck in the old pure "reengineering the corporation" approach advocated by Hammer and Champy two decades ago, without adding two additional steps that are necessary in this design (despite the fact that even Michael Hammer eventually adopted the combined approach as ERP platforms became more competent):[2]

- Understanding the business processes that are native to whatever enterprise platform has been selected.
- Selecting native approaches that meet the objectives of process designs, unless the business benefits support the adoption of non-native processes.

At times, evaluation of approaches to business design issues may also be part of the evaluation and selection process. In either case, this cannot be a simple investigation of a list of processes or practices considered "best" but must be based on extensive business process knowledge within the ERP system. Although this knowledge is difficult to find, it is a crucial component of the evaluation. Some ERP vendors have courses that provide this education; others do not. Gaining this knowledge, however, will prove to be a critical key to success or failure.

SKILLS TO INCLUDE

Once you have adopted an approach to this analysis, the skill areas that must be possessed by the design team include

- Business knowledge
- IT applications process knowledge
- Knowledge of native business processes in the ERP application
- Training in process thinking

Once this is done, it becomes an issue of how to manage the program effectively, which will be addressed in Chapters 10 and 11 dealing with governance and organizational change management. Let's investigate each of the four skills areas in greater depth.

Business Knowledge

Frequently, business methods or processes have evolved over many years, and current managers, while they may know how to operate their part of the processes, really don't understand how they integrate with other components of the business. There is a large difference between knowing how to do something and understanding why you are doing it or, for that matter, what effects your actions may have on others. In many businesses, as the organization has developed and expanded over the years and the people who developed current work procedures moved on or left the business, no one has taken the time to explain to new workers the "what, how, or why" of performing the tasks that they are doing. In fact, new employees will continue to solve problems by ad hoc redesign of business process components, not knowing how the current systems work. Typically, this ad hoc redesigning of business processes gets worse over the years unless concerted efforts are made to reverse the process.

Unless the current managers have taken responsibility for their work area, processes, and procedures, it is very likely that the company itself may not have sufficient knowledge of how the business operates to properly design new systems. Again, we are not indicating that the functional departments are not competent to perform their functions the way they were designed, just that knowledge of why they operate the way they do has, in many cases, been lost.

While leading a large number of business process reengineering studies some years ago, we found that very involved and committed workers were exhausted from suggesting changes to the systems they operated on. In this case, in particular, several businesses were operating on the same set of legacy applications, so that changes that were important to one of the divisions would also have a significant impact on other divisions that didn't have the same issues or, more often, had different but equally problematic concerns. Unlike ERP systems, where many business process designs are specific to one organizational unit or another, these functions were often shared, and changes could occur when only all divisions agreed to a new design, which was difficult. Over the years, this had institutionalized the status quo and prevented any serious attempt to improve overall system and business performance. As easy as it is to simply blame the IT department, in this case, the IT department was completely hamstrung and could not have made most of the changes anyway. In this environment, folks had simply given up looking at the business process and continued to do what was necessary to get transactions completed. Over time, the knowledge of the business process became even more remote. During reengineering studies, simple discussions (or debates) over how even simple components actually operated could take hours and at times never reach agreement.

An enterprise that doesn't have fundamental process knowledge to define where its current weak points are is particularly at risk and should undertake a program to define the current state before undertaking any transformation process. This may be incorporated into a front-end study or can be developed prior to starting. You will hear that a business would like to skip this step so as not to focus on the past but to point to the future; however, the knowledge gained by understanding how and why current business processes work the way they do is a key to designing improved processes that will still address valid challenges from the past. Although this can be overdone, knowing where you have come from can help determine where you are going.

It is also a long-term process and one that must be sustained over time to keep the enterprise healthy. There are many business analysis techniques that have evolved over the years, some of which are tied to specific packages, but cross-functional discussions that can lead to understanding current business processes can be used to at least define the current situation. If you start to design a new process without understanding current processes, you will inevitably make oversights or, even worse, make avoidable errors in the new design. As a word of caution, it is also necessary to avoid getting ahead of the study process and start designing before you understand the current processes thoroughly.

IT Applications Process Knowledge

Let's assume that we have or have created sufficient current business knowledge. This does not imply that it includes understanding how current applications work in support of the processes. Current process understanding, incidentally, is necessary in both legacy systems and organizations with ERP packages that may not have done the work of completing the transformation. We are not suggesting that business leaders need to understand the technology (programming or configuration) itself. For example, in the early days of implementing ERP, the sales order processing capabilities of integrated platforms would be designed to simplify the job of an order entry representative by populating master data information on the customer, the products, the pricing, and perhaps even the availability. Previously, we discussed a situation where a single application supported multiple business divisions in which many of the business processes were shared by many or all of the divisions. In this case, the application was rarely a process that any one business had designed but was a poor compromise across divisions and decades. It is crucial to understand not only the business processes, including desktop work, that are done in a business, but also the logic of the actual IT applications that integrate (or interface) between back-office functions.[3] This investigation need not delve into detail around "how" and "why" but should define the "what" of how these business processes—essential in later chapters as we consider culture, politics, and organizational change challenges—operate. This knowledge will become crucial in designing the transition to new integrated processes.

Native Business Processes in the ERP Application

As much as organizations often don't do the work to understand their current systems, many ERP implementations proceed without sufficient knowledge of the possibilities or potential in the new systems, either. This applies both to client project teams and to consulting teams. This relegates the design process to a discussion of repeating the current design (the only thing the client knows) or implementing a process that the consultants happen to know (limited to what the consultants have experienced). Native business processes supported in any of the modern ERP platforms are an area of knowledge where specific attention must be paid. If you relegate process design to only those solutions that team has experienced and combine that with insufficient knowledge of current business needs, it is difficult to see how optimal solutions can ever be achieved except by chance, which is an uncertain strategy at best.

In instance after instance, someone may suggest a solution to a business process design issue, only to be told that "the ERP system doesn't do it that way." While this may be true, it is always necessary to test this premise by asking why the ERP system won't do it that way. A team should never accept that it simply won't.[4] If the designer cannot articulate why it won't, the odds are pretty good that either it actually will and the consultant doesn't know how, or that learning the logic of why it can't be done a certain way opens up insight into other ways in which it can be done more simply to accomplish the same outcome. Remember that we are learning the logic of business relationships and designing an application to help us manage these relationships—not adopting some arbitrary design without a logical foundation.

In many large implementations, the fundamental element of knowledge missing is cross-functional business process knowledge within the ERP system, both in the business and consulting workforces. The nature of both client business organizations and consulting organizations is to develop extremely deep functional knowledge, with little attention paid to cross-functional understanding.[5] This is a recipe for disaster and often leads to decisions to modify ERP software to repeat current business processes, virtually ensuring that organizational results will not change. At the start of a program or a design of a continuous improvement program, as this book recommends, a first requirement is to ensure that the project team and the leadership have access to people who know the native cross-functional processes that exist in the new system. Once you know that something is possible, finding someone who knows how to configure or program it is easy. Without this knowledge, most project outcomes are less than optimal or downright disastrous.

Training in Process Thinking

Process thinking is a discipline, and this is why a road map to learning this discipline is emphasized in the Preface. Typically, one does not set out to learn this perspective, but the story is illustrative of how the thought process and methodology are developed. The ability to see the relationship between components of the system (or different departments) is the key to under-standing how any business operates and therefore how to resolve design issues. Another example is flying an airplane. The ability to fly and control an airplane is dependent on many different components, including ailerons, elevators, rudders, flaps, and propulsion systems, among many others. While all of these components are integrated and managed by computers, it doesn't change the fact that understanding all of these as individual points won't get an airplane in the air. Rather, it is in understanding the relationship and interactions between the pieces that leads to successful flight. When some-thing in an airplane malfunctions, as in the case of the airliner that landed in New York City's Hudson River, the knowledge of the relationships among all of the flight control surfaces is critical to safely resolving the issue.

It is much the same in business. Is high inventory a result of a poor sales forecast in general, a poor prediction of the effect of trade promotions, poor production scheduling, poor warehouse management, customer returns, or many others? Just as with the airplane, the answer lies not in one or another of these but in the interaction of all of them. In staff meeting after staff meeting, the discussion/debate is over which to blame for the poor result, when the answer has to be addressed by process understanding. Furthermore, addressing one touch point without understanding the business process that determines the final result inevitably leads to unintended consequences and further conflict. In all likelihood, these actions have resulted in the challenge afflicting the organization today. As mentioned earlier, one of the fundamental precepts of Dr. W. Edwards Deming was that all business failures result from defective business processes and that blaming hapless workers is never an effective cor-rective action. The same adage applies to single elements of business processes. Though clearly not a universal truth, it rings true much more often than not.

A PLAN FOR ACTION

So, how do we do all of this? In order to be successful in producing improved business results, all of these components must be evaluated. Business process knowledge doesn't just happen, and knowledge of how work processes and IT applications work together to produce business results is rarely part of current business education programs, but it is integral to our learning experience. There are many tools to assist us in developing this knowledge, from simple (but thorough) business process mapping approaches to complex business process management (BPM) tools that may incorporate many other technologies (Six Sigma, lean manufacturing or "lean whatever," statistical quality control, and others). For knowledge of business processes in SAP, a leading ERP program, for example, there is Business Process Integration Certification (TERP 10), which teaches cross-functional business processes that are defined across all of the ERP functions in the product, both functional and technical. Other ERP providers have courses that address the same need. When dealing with enterprise platforms (remember that we defined this as the collection of business applications that the corporation operates on) that consist of more than one package, this need becomes even greater. Mapping business processes across multiple platforms is also valuable when making a decision on which software packages to use.

Whatever the approach, it is important to manage this formally with a program to collect knowledge of the business's current and future state, define necessary changes, evaluate the organizational impact, and execute programs to manage the transition. This is part of all successful implementation programs today. Chapter 11 specifically describes a process to manage this, both with the departments being impacted and with leaders. For this part of the discussion, suffice it to say that it is necessary to define current and future states; evaluate and collect all of the changes that will affect the organization, including skill set transition; combine everything into focus group and communication programs; and ultimately deliver it through various training programs. The actual work of designing the new processes will be done later by the project team members, typically using tools that are part of the selected package. Deciding how the analytical and design process will be managed and ensuring that the necessary skills are available are crucial as part of preparing to design the business processes that will ultimately determine future business results.

SUMMARY

The work product of business process analysis is a list of the errors, the inefficiencies, and the actions that are necessary to resolve current business process problems, as well as an identification of how these issues will be addressed in the new enterprise applications platform. If this is part of the ERP platform, then the outcomes and process designs should be consistent with the logic and capabilities of the package selected. If the process cannot be delivered in the new platform but will instead be delivered in another package or modification of the ERP platform, it should be accompanied by a clear definition of what particular function(s) cannot be delivered by the standard platform, as well as by an estimate of the additional cost for modifications versus intended additional benefits. All of these modifications or the use of additional platforms should result in benefits that are greater than the cost within the standard process solutions in the base ERP package, the same way that any other business expenditure is evaluated.

Often this analysis is done during ERP implementations in the stage called a blueprint or design phase, and documentation tools are used during that phase of the project to gather and record information on individual process designs. Because many issues that will occur during the later project phases will ultimately be the result of cultural, political, strategic, or educational conflicts with the intended designs, much of this initial process must be done at an earlier stage of the program, such that the final continuous business improvement plans will also include other elements of the program. Finding the right balance between the general design process that is needed at this early stage and the detailed work done later in the program, once it has been accepted, is the key to success.

 NOTES

1. Marvin R. Weisbord, *Productive Workplaces: Dignity, Meaning, and Community in the 21st Century* (San Francisco: Jossey-Bass, 1987).
2. Michael Hammer and James Champy, *Re-engineering the Corporation: A Manifesto for Business Revolution* (New York: Harper Business Essentials, 1993).
3. Andrew Spanyi, *More for Less: The Power of Process Management* (Tampa: Meghan-Kiffer Press, 2007).
4. Andrew Spanyi, *Business Process Management Is a Team Sport* (Tampa: Anclote Press, 2003).
5. Andrew Spanyi, *Operational Leadership* (New York: Business Expert Press, 2010).

CHAPTER SIX

Business Culture, Politics, and Organization

"Consultants, industrial salespeople, and others who regularly see firms up close without being employees know well how much culture operates outside of people's awareness, even rather visibly unusual aspects of a culture. . . . Because corporate culture exerts this kind of influence, the new practices created in a reengineering or a restructuring or an acquisition must somehow be anchored in it; if not, they can be very fragile and subject to regression."

—*John Kotter*, Leading Change

 ## INTRODUCTION

It is customary when discussing implementation approaches and the need to manage change during projects to include the role of corporate culture, either in assisting or, more often, in resisting changes. These discussions often refer to culture as "bad" or, even worse, as something to be overcome. The same, unfortunately, is often said of company politics and organizational structures.

Although this may be the way in which they are seen to manifest, an enterprise's culture, politics, and organization are as natural to its existence and performance as business processes are.

 ## CULTURAL BARRIERS AND ENABLERS

Can you imagine a business without a culture, a political structure, or an organizational concept? These have grown up with the company and are inevitable characteristics of any organization. All human organizations have them, but we tend to see them only when we believe that one of these characteristics is preventing us from achieving our objectives. Once understood, businesses often look for magic bullets to deal with these aspects of the enterprise and focus only on overcoming resistance to change that may be exhibited. This negative-only view helps create a fatalistic view of their impact on program performance.

Rather than working to overcome these, all three should be considered a natural part of any organization, and they can and should be used to facilitate changes and to drive the search for more business value. This, however, requires that leadership acknowledge this complex issue as one that requires thought, design, buy-in, and continuous support to be successful. As a corollary of this, businesses must also consider opportunities to promote education to develop understanding of how they can be used constructively in the company. Too often, instead, businesses look for "Salvation in a Box" and buy into trendy current programs, without putting work into understanding the current cultural, political, and organizational realities, issues (both positive and negative to change), and opportunities to apply the principals involved, rather than just formulas, in order to achieve results. It is not that there aren't great concepts and approaches embedded in today's consulting toolsets, but it is adapting these concepts to a specific situation that allows the leadership team to use these factors to create value. Some years ago, Dr. Joseph Juran (quality guru and founder of the American Society of Quality Control Engineers) described another quality program package as "a pretty package. When you open a package, however, there should be something of value inside of it" (from a discussion held during Dr. Juran's final seminar series—"The Last Word"— in 1994).

When leading ERP-driven business transformation programs, one often hears answers such as

- "You don't understand how political the executive organization is."
- "We have a really messed up culture, and it will never work."
- "This is one confused organization, and we cannot succeed unless it changes."

All of these statements express frustrations with what team members perceive as roadblocks to success. Yet they are also predictable excuses that allow planning for failure, an attribute that is also often part of corporate culture. Let's establish, through the following discussions, a couple of principles:

- First, all groups of two of more people who work together to try to accomplish goals adopt a culture, a political relationship, and an organizing structure of some sort—all groups, even a group as personal as a marriage. Although some groups may well be described as "bad," based on some standard, the fact is that very few groups are "bad," in and of themselves, and most groups can be used constructively to get work done once one understands how groups work. The questions to be asked are "What are we going to do to understand the cultural, political, and organizational realities?" and "How will we use this information to accomplish our goals?" rather than asking how to overcome bad culture, politics, or organization.
- Second, one needs to learn about and avoid the Salvation in a Box syndrome, the tendency to depend on packaged solutions that are not well designed to resolve the issues that need to be addressed. Salvation in a Box should be avoided by understanding the current situation and selecting individual ideas and concepts that are assembled in a manner that best serves the group's purposes. A consultant offering solutions wrapped in a pretty package, with great slide-ware supporting it, cannot be effective if the solutions are not perfectly aligned with the current situation. This rarely, if ever, occurs without effort and typically results in what the organization derisively refers to as the "program du jour." Program du jour can best be described as many employees who feel exhausted from change and are reacting to the syndrome of too much perception of change and too little actual change, In other words, "too much work for too little reward."

As an example, a large organization was adopting the Crosby Quality Program to improve overall product and organizational quality and required each business segment to adopt the 14-step process recommended by Crosby.

Quarterly reports were required on which step the organization was engaged in. One plant routinely reported something like steps 3, 6, 7, 9, and 10 but was told that it was supposed to perform the steps one at a time in sequence. It kept reporting this way and was routinely criticized for it. Yet it was awarded the business quality program award each year for three years. This is simply an example of a company adopting a Salvation in a Box approach without understanding the organizational elements that were being changed. It also shows that doing the work of actually delivering the program focused on results can change the results.

KEYS TO UNDERSTANDING CULTURE, POLITICS, AND ORGANIZATION

Certain key areas need to be analyzed and addressed in planning programs. Although there are more, the following six areas lead to understanding and developing keys to success:

1. Executive barriers
2. Destructive incentives
3. Origins of the current design
4. I am what I lead
5. Levels of empowerment
6. Mean time to change one's mind

Executive Barriers

Chris Argyris, in his book *Overcoming Organizational Defenses*, identifies reasons that groups of high-performing leaders become dysfunctional as executive staff groups.[1] Frequently, executives come to consider their current positions as the culmination of their careers. They have risen through single functions, become recognized as the best in their career fields, and possess unassailable knowledge of their aspect of the business. These executives have adopted rigid attitudes toward business process changes that affect their areas, and without special attention to define the costs and benefits of changes to the organization as a whole, they will continue to focus only on their areas of expertise. They have strongly formed ideas about what works and what doesn't because their ideas have been reinforced by past success and are almost always from the perspective of metrics for which they have been responsible. In addition, these executives see themselves in competition for future promotions or increases in responsibility. They also know they can win in this competition by demonstrating leadership and their ability to formulate policies and processes that achieve their personal objectives. Their departmental programs are often in conflict with those of other leaders and can be the subject of continuous friction in executive suite discussions.

Far from being a problem in normal times, this may bring strength to the enterprise. The problem, however, is that in order to fully achieve the potential benefits of business process changes with ERP implementations, it is necessary for these executives to work as a group and agree on cross-functional designs to achieve the greatest Return on Investment for the company. This flies directly in the face of what has made these executives successful and, in many cases, requires them to abandon winning approaches from the past and collaborate on designs that provide less value to their departments but contribute more to the broader organization.

Here is where leadership principles discussed in Chapter 2 can be demonstrated. As part of the vision a leader creates, it is necessary to either include the organizational behaviors necessary to achieve the intended changes, or leaders must ensure that knowledge of cross-functional relationships is available to the executive team. This must be a part of a governance process to help executive leadership make or support process design decisions to keep the program on track for cost, timing, and benefits.

Destructive Incentives

All organizations have incentives for management (top level, or extending deep into the organization) that reward desired behaviors. Even when these are not directly tied to compensation, performance against them is recorded in appraisals that directly affect promotions or other assignments. Often, however, even tools or plans that are well conceived and managed can create barriers to the successful implementation of new business processes in ERP programs. When seemingly good individual objectives create situations where there are winners and losers, these objectives can be called "destructive incentives." At first, this may sound like something that rarely occurs, but, unfortunately, these unintended consequences of incentive programs are quite common. The following examples of intended or unintended consequences of incentive programs will illustrate the point.

▪ The first example is intentional and usually misguided. In this scenario, the incentives and directions are purposefully created as part of a management style to pit two departmental executives against each other, under the belief that conflict is a good caldron to force creative solutions. In some cases, the technique is used to disguise the fact that leaders creating the situation are not sure what the solution should be and want to prevent one faction from becoming too strong, thus using this to reinforce their own position. In one example, a senior executive appointed both the COO and the CIO of a subsidiary business at the same time, telling each that his success was dependent on not letting the other function design the new products but holding each responsible. Rather than creating a cauldron of creative thinking, this created myopic political camps whose members routinely worked to prevent the other camp from being successful. The results were disastrous; the product was never successfully completed, even after years and millions of dollars of investment. This is an extreme but important example of the reason that projects fail for lack of top leadership support. Yet elements of this lack of support are quite common when the need for cross-functional knowledge is not acknowledged and addressed. If this technique is being used, the Program Governance Office, described later in this book, must intervene, pointing out the conflict and getting it resolved so that incentives and directions are clear and consistent with each other. If this cannot be achieved, there is little point in continuing with the program.

▪ The next example is less confrontational but can be even more difficult to detect or resolve. It is common for procurement functions to have incentives to reduce purchasing costs. Because most companies have a "standard cost" for inventoried materials, incentives are typically expressed as "positive purchase price variance," meaning that goods are procured at below standard costs. On the other hand, manufacturing incentives often reward reduction of raw material inventories in order to reduce working capital, thus saving on the cost of inventory. The problem or the confrontation occurs because one of the primary means of reducing the purchase price is by increasing order quantities, which creates additional inventory. This natural pressure between the two functions is exacerbated by the implementation of ERP systems where a single cross-functional business process is designed and installed. To effectively produce maximum business value, an organization might create a material control function with an incentive based on the total cost of inventory, which includes both purchase price and inventory. It should be noted that there are also other factors in play here, but the illustration is accurate.

There are countless examples of the law of unintended consequences that must be dealt with when implementing changes required by conversion to an integration business system. It requires leaders and decision makers who have a broader knowledge of how organizations and business processes work cross-functionally, not merely a skill set that occurs by accident. Cultural norms, such as incentive systems, must be considered as management tools that may have to be reworked, regardless of how politically sensitive it may be to do so.

Finally, project team members who report to and represent functional leaders cannot be expected to fight for solutions that are going to adversely affect their leader and themselves if these issues cannot be identified and addressed. Because this involves objectives, variable compensations, and potential promotions, the restructuring of these incentives to get rid of destructive elements is a function that must be dealt with through a governance program such as the one described in Chapter 10.

Origins of the Current Design

It is easy to neglect the "how and who" of the current situation, but it is a reasonable assumption that the current set of processes was defined and built by someone who "owns" current designs. This individual may have even been promoted or otherwise incentivized for that design. Now this person must be brought on board with impending changes or, in some cases, replaced. The assumption with ERP teams typically is that the existing business processes and IT applications are not competent, are not properly operated, and/or simply can be ignored in the future design. Although some version of this perception may be true, there is a lot to be learned about the business, that is, how it developed and what problem the IT systems were designed to resolve. In addition, incumbent managers in both functional areas and IT started out to solve problems, and, over the years, development simply built on the original logic to the point where it was necessary to start over. Even SAP (the largest ERP vendor in the market) has had many restarts in its history. SAP started with R/2, then developed R/3; next came the development of BAPIs (business application program interfaces), Business Suite, Netweaver, and so on. So, the thought that homegrown solutions should have been able to foresee the technology and business evolution over the years is usually incorrect. This doesn't change, however, the fact that the original designers or owners of the existing processes will feel attacked unless they are included in the solution. The net result is that for both learning and team building, the current set of business processes and IT applications needs to be included so that the designers of the new system understand the history of the processes and IT applications.

There is often a level of arrogance in ERP consultants who are tasked with replacing existing systems, a level of arrogance that is generally counterproductive. This intersection between proud process designer/owners and consultants who have seen a new and better way can be a source of significant organizational pain. This is made worse by the level of educational understanding and knowledge that team members (client and consultants) bring to the program. This will be directly addressed in detail in Chapter 8. Also, industry leaders have not effectively defined the set of business skills that should be included in any ERP consultant's educational process. This is no longer a purely IT project; it is a business project using IT applications to drive business improvements. Project teams need to consider themselves as business teams using IT and not the other way around, and this requires a different educational background. Without this business and human process knowledge in the consultant workforce, the client organization must establish a function within the governance process to ensure that this is addressed and controlled, not only defensively, but to assure optimal process design.

Another reason this occurs is that it is easier to simply dismiss the current processes than it is to learn why they are the way they are. Much of what Charlie Feld (the former CEO of the Feld Group and the former SEVP of EDS) refers to as a "hairball" legacy program is actually the sequential implementation of functional fixes without understanding the unintended consequences to other functions of the business. Mr. Feld has been frustrated by the explosion of legacy applications that have grown layer upon layer over the years, often without adequate documentation of additional layers or corrections made in the underlying code. Companies have tended to make seemingly endless tweaks to the existing systems, which made the situation even more precarious. He argues that this endless tweaking is dangerous and fails to take advantage of the capability of modern applications, whether ERP or hybrid platforms, built on service oriented architecture.

Understanding the design of these legacy applications can provide insight into business solutions that were developed to satisfy a problem or need, and most likely, the solutions still exist. Understanding these needs and the history behind the processes is key to understanding the business issues involved and untangling them during implementation. This approach, however, requires analytical work to create understanding at a level of detail that few project teams or client teams are prepared to tackle. There is probably no better predictor of failure than to neglect, as well as not to understand, existing processes. Clients and consultants must understand the reasons for the current processes, the problems they were designed to resolve, and the need to engage the owners in the designing of new processes. It is a modern-day business-focused version of "those who cannot remember the past are condemned to repeat it."[2]

I Am What I Lead

Another challenge encountered with leaders is the self-belief that they "are what they do." This leads to the belief that their status in the organization is directly dependent on how many employees, functions, budget dollars, and so on, they have direct responsibility for. Moving from functionally developed processes to cross-functional business processes will, by necessity, result in the consolidation of some functions where the pieces currently report to different leaders. This may cause one leader to be seen as "gaining" in prestige at the expense of others. Psychologists encourage us to think about our personal worth as our abilities, contributions, and values and not as what we do. This is often not the reality. A classic example is customer service representatives who take pride in their relationships with customers because they can find information on individuals, locations, products, and so on, that personalize the experience and the relationship between customer and client. ERP comes in and their job becomes data entry and reporting back the results of the transaction that may include all of the information that was part of their relationship. While providing more to the customer, this change challenges the representative's self-image as providing human value to the customer. We all resist changes that are seen as devaluing our personal worth or sense of self. This is a simple example, but with leaders, it can be even more insidious.

Some of the most intractable disagreements come when functions are being combined and assigned to one leader to the perceived detriment of another. In one instance, a reorganization of roles and responsibilities within a staff group was going to result in a significant reduction in the responsibilities of one of the leaders. The reorganization was necessitated by a redesign of business processes. After lengthy discussions, it became obvious that this individual believed that he was being put in a position he was uncomfortable with and that his resistance to the changes was the result of a loss of "self" that would occur (he no longer would report on the division staff). In this case, the roles, responsibilities, and influence of the leader were being adjusted, but his ability to influence the organization or compensation was not diminished. Resistance came solely from the perceived loss of the "staff member" prestige. Some businesses seem to have designed this into their corporate cultures, and while it may have started innocuously, it can become a key criterion of influence in the business.

In another example, while we worked to transform a functional organization from being a collection of small vertical disconnected pieces all doing the same thing but using different procedures, the issue was not whether the organizational logic made any sense, but it was simply the perceived loss of control in the departments. Therefore, influence was lost in the larger organization, despite the fact that the adoption of standard procedures (this was a quality assurance function) and the combination of staff resulted in an improved consistency of results, improved overall product quality, and increased productivity by more than 50 percent. Often, the way that yearly departmental objectives are set institutionalizes this in businesses when compensating through performance incentives. The issue is not only the individual self-perceptions but how they have been encouraged and institutionalized by management processes as well.

Levels of Empowerment

There are empowerment dynamics within implementation project teams and between the teams and their parent departments. These dynamics determine how decision making and issue resolution will be managed and timeliness enforced. This is tied to culture, as well as to individual leader personalities, meaning that even in cultures where empowerment extends deep into the organization, individual leaders may not embrace this as part of their leadership style. Having a grand meeting where everyone agrees to see that decisions are made in a timely fashion without fully understanding the decision-making standards implicit in the culture is akin to deciding to change your lottery luck by wishing harder. This process has to be designed and defined within the culture it will live within and promoted throughout the organization. If, for example, department leaders are determined to make all process decisions by themselves, they by de facto put themselves on the project team, with proxies doing the hour-to-hour work. It must be clearly explained that the manager will have to be available full time, as needed, to make design decisions and resolve interdepartmental design conflicts. It simply cannot be otherwise, or the program will not stay on time and budget.

Years ago, while designing a chemical plant, the project team had a well-developed and thorough project plan that included a well-constructed "critical path" analysis. In other words, the team knew what decisions had to be made by certain dates in order to keep the overall project on time—things such as reactor vessels arriving before the roof was put on the plant so that they could be dropped into the structures. Due to vendor, installation, and commissioning lead times, the project leaders knew exactly when vendor selection had to be determined; however, there was disagreement between the two top program leaders on the selection.

When the final date arrived for the decision to be made (according to the critical path), the two leaders still could not find agreement and started to defer the decision for another week. The obvious, but rarely asked, question that was posed was, "What was the spending authorization level for these two leaders?" In other words, how much could they authorize on their own signatures? The answer was $25,000. Their problem was that the weekly spend on the project teams was $250,000 for all of the engineers, the program leaders, the construction crews, and others. If you have developed detailed, believable critical path documents, and the team has accepted them, this argument is valid and can be used to drive decision making. In this case, the decision was made on time, and the project stayed on schedule. The point of this story is that it is crucial as one analyzes the business culture of the organization to understand how decisions are made, who can authorize what, and how to resolve issues that will negatively affect the project at the outset. Although this can be a highly political discussion, it is actually pretty straightforward and one that must be included in the assessment of the levels of empowerment.

Mean Time to Change One's Mind

This is always a sensitive issue, because no management team wants to be faced with the effects of leadership changes and how these changes may derail project plans. Why is this event, the change in leadership, a concern? When was the last time that your organization went two years (or some other period of time) without changing a senior leader [CxO] or various VP levels)? The answer is very likely "never." Assuming this is the case and your project timeline is longer than two years, the next logical question is, "When was the last time your organization hired a new executive with the expectation that the new executive would not change anything, that the new executive would just run the organization as it is currently?" Again, the answer is inevitably "never." When organizations recruit to replace leaders, they are looking for candidates with outstanding track records who can bring new approaches and programs to the position. These new approaches and programs will be identical to current processes only by accident.

There are three questions concerning executive transitions that need to be assessed to understand the cultural impact on project planning:

1. How will the organization transition to new leaders without derailing the program stream?
2. Will the continuous improvement program and governance processes be acceptable to the new executives as they put their stamp on their contribution?
3. What is the process for introducing the new executives into the governance process that is overseeing and guiding the program?

In other words, how can expectations be set for managing executive transitions that will inevitably occur during the project or projects?

Furthermore, analyzing a typical cycle of management support can provide good input into how small the increments a program stream is broken into. If new leadership will be focused on reviewing only the program stream not already in progress with the understanding that current projects will continue to completion and be expected to achieve the planned results, then you can use the Program Governance Office to shield current projects from this rethinking process. Otherwise, you will end up with a constant rethinking that can euphemistically be called navel gazing (the tendency to figuratively stare at one's navel, when frozen by fear), which creates uncertainty in the organization and often results in failure. You just have to look at large programs that are years into the implementation cycle. To see how important this principle is, the majority of these large implementation programs have been restarted numerous times and, in many cases, are no closer to success than when they started. Although you may expect new executives to allow a project to run a few months without changes, it is not reasonable to expect that the new executives will not want to set their own direction for a matter of years. It is necessary to construct individual projects that can be completed within the mean time for your organization to change its mind.

COMPILING INSIGHTS GAINED

While all very interesting and obviously somewhat subjective, what can be used to create action-ready programs, either to manage within the existing culture or to include in some transition of cultural norms as the major program progresses? First, it is necessary to fully understand how the organization views leadership, variable compensation programs, organizational structures, and political relationships. A political relationship is the culture either of negotiation between functional leaders or of collaboration between leaders where objectives are more shared. Although these organizational views may be difficult to discuss in leadership groups, the output from these conversations is absolutely essential to understand the impact on the governance program you will develop to manage longer-term continuous improvement programs. Many books on the market discuss how to reform "problematic cultures," as well as how to move the cultural idiom of companies to one based on some principle. There are coaching programs, team-building programs, and more. All of these are valuable in some circumstances and superficial in others.

The intent of this discussion is not to talk about tools that can be used to design and execute cultural transformations, but to discuss and develop an understanding of how cultural characteristics of an enterprise affect the ability to successfully execute continuous improvement programs, keep them focused on return on investment, and resolve issues as they arise. If this analysis results in some realizations about how these aspects of culture can have a negative effect on organizational performance, the executive group may want to adopt organizational development programs to address this and other issues, but that is not the intent here. For our purposes, we need to understand how the organization handles each of these aspects, evaluates how this can or will affect the stability and focus on the programs moving forward, and states in clear and actionable terms what aspects of managing this process must be incorporated into a governance program. In addition, other culture modification programs may have to also be a part of this process if they are conducted at the same time.

 ## RELATING THESE INSIGHTS TO THE PROJECT ITSELF

The working corporate culture has an impact on several important aspects of creating project teams responsible to design and implement improved business processes. This relates both to program design and to project management. The level of understanding of the elements needed to manage projects to achieve successful realization of business results must be an important consideration for building project teams. More typically, client project team members are selected for their knowledge of the functional areas they represent, rather than for their knowledge of how to analyze and deliver business results. Tragically, the most qualified people are designated as "too valuable to lose" (again, a product of the culture), and consequently, members assigned to the team are those who are more easily replaceable. Regardless, these more replaceable people will still determine the future financial success of the organization. This is not intended to disparage conscientious people assigned to the team, but to point out that leaders need to ensure that their representatives are truly the ones they would want designing their future success or failure.

Some years ago, a business attempted an implementation of MRP II and asked three departments (sales, production planning, and manufacturing) to assign individuals to work on the project full time. Although each of the workers assigned was smart, understood his or her function, and was committed, none of them had sufficient credibility with the rest of the organization to gain support. Each department had deemed workers better equipped to gain support as too important to lose. The result was that the project significantly overran the budget, both for time and for costs, and ultimately was never completed successfully. It is important to point out that none of the workers assigned were bad or not committed to the project. In this case, the appointments needed to be made while recognizing the organizational culture, and the people who had the credibility and the support within the organization to get it done successfully should have been assigned. Selecting the proper people to assign is as much an art as a science, but a company must take into consideration the ability to lead and gain support from the organization.

A healthy organization often has established programs to continuously build knowledge and competency around how to assess the details of organizational and process design that ultimately determine results, and these people will play key roles, not only in the ERP design, but ultimately in all business process decisions. These employees will see their roles as being master mechanics of the organization, on both the cultural and the applications level. In these roles, they typically continue to gain knowledge of current states, relationships within the organization, and the tools that can be used to manage a continuous improvement process at all levels. This is not a "special" skill set but one that must be incorporated into organizational expectations. Although the organization may use a contractor to meet immediate needs, the roles of master mechanics of the organization need to be developed by the organization as a planned competency.

SUMMARY

This process of establishing base-level understanding of the existing culture, any proposed changes to decision-making processes, incorporation into the governance program, and/or planning for future executive transitions will be key to achieving intended business results. It should also be noted that while the continuous improvement programs will continue over time, it is necessary to ensure that this analysis remains "green." This means that as the culture changes, business processes change, reorganizations occur, and leadership changes, the analysis must be updated to ensure that there are not new challenges being created. Remember that just as manufacturing and sales processes are part of any business, so are culture, political, and organizational structures. They must be understood and managed for ERP programs to be successful and produce the maximum potential return on investment.

NOTES

1. Chris Argyris, *Overcoming Organizational Defenses: Facilitating Organizational Learning* (Needham Heights, MA: Allyn and Bacon, 1990).
2. George Santayana, *Reason in Common Sense: The Life of Reason* (New York: Charles Scribner's Sons, 1905).

7

IT Strategy Review

"Senior business executives lack a well-established management process for taking charge of IT. Business managers consequently have not developed the kind of experience and expertise in IT that they have in finance, human resources, and accounting."

—*Peter G. W. Keen,* Shaping the Future

 INTRODUCTION

IT planning is often thought of as being more tactical than strategic. Yet IT strategy done properly drives investment, sets expectations, and can either enable or hinder the ability of an organization to change. The role of IT strategy development must be discussed specifically. IT strategy development determines how effective continuous improvement programs will be in a business using ERP platforms or any other integrated business applications suite; this is a key discussion to have when evaluating approaches to IT-driven business improvement programs. Like all staff functions in a business, IT is often considered only a support function, with internally focused sets of goals and objectives, rather than a function that operates at the execution layer of all other departments.

In addition, IT is often seen as an unfortunate cost to the organization, and when IT is involved in significant projects, many think IT causes a lot of pain, which is something to be endured or avoided. This is a legacy of the early days of the discipline, where nearly all IT skill sets were very technical in nature and required extensive technical education. As IT applications have become more user-friendly and more powerful in delivering functional support to business, IT's position in the organization has not changed very much to reflect changes in its ability to influence business results, as described in Chapter 3.

AN EXAMPLE OF A FLAWED IT STRATEGY

The previously mentioned view has existed for a couple of decades, as the following example demonstrates. The business in question had appeared to be profitable for many years. In recent years, however, the business began to show rapidly declining profit, stagnant sales, and product quality issues. A team was assigned to turn this situation around, yet at every turn, as attempts were made to change the internal dynamics of the organization, the standard response was "the systems don't do it that way." This applied to the way finished goods inventory was stored and managed, how customer orders were processed and filled, how production planning evaluated the demand on manufacturing, how manufacturing capacity was applied, and many more areas. The strategy of the business up to that time had been to invest as little as needed to develop functionality in support of the business's ability to perform transactions, collect the records of the transactions, and report financials.

In the ensuing several years, during which the organization was successful in restructuring, improving productivity, reducing working capital, and returning to profitability, IT strategy was revised significantly. An evaluation of all of the core business processes was conducted, the relationship between various components defined, business process owners established, new functional design specifications written, legacy program technical specifications written jointly between process owners (business leaders) and IT, and projects sequenced and executed. All were based on a significant and well-established Return on Investment program. During a period of thirty months, the headcount in core departments was reduced by 60 percent, total inventory was cut by 60 percent, back orders decreased from $2.5M to less than $200K, and product quality improved such that the market share was once again growing and the business was profitable.

One of the key components of the program was a dramatic revision of the IT strategy for this business. In deciding how to address financial challenges within the business, a philosophical change occurred. IT strategy changed from one of managing a perpetual series of work orders based on minimizing the amount spent on these programs to an aggressive rewrite of functionality, based on well-defined and executed Return on Investment cases. To facilitate this process, departments were temporarily reorganized, such that all internal logistics and manufacturing support functions reported to a shared services director. This leader became the de facto business process owner; however, day-to-day analysis, design, testing, and implementation responsibilities were delegated to department managers. These projects were planned to run sequentially during the turnaround period. This was all in the years just prior to the practical introduction of ERP programs being made available to smaller and mid-size businesses. Yet the story is a dramatic example of how IT strategy can dramatically affect business results. The move from cost avoidance and dreaded periodic projects to planned sequential investment based on expected Return on Investment was a key component of the successful business turnaround.

It is also interesting to consider what happened after the results were achieved. Subsequent to the "completion" of the turnaround program, the core business leader and IT leadership held a strategy development session and developed a Return on Investment–based program to continue funding a series of IT development projects, all of which would be based on a demonstrated ability to deliver Return on Investment for these programs. Despite the two-and-a-half-year track record of successful returns, the business decided to take a different course and moved back to the practice of treating IT as an unfortunate but necessary cost of doing business and rejected the strategy proposed by the core business departments. Even in this case, where a different approach to IT strategy was used and had demonstrated its power to turn the business results around, reversion to short-term tactical approaches was again taken. The needed commitment to long-term continuous improvement, driven by optimization programs using IT applications, was never adopted because the organization never associated the immediate benefits with the ability to continue to provide longer-term transformational results. Not surprisingly,

business improvements as a result of previous work done continued to posi-
tively affect results; however, significant additional business benefit was left
untouched.

WHAT THE INTRODUCTION OF ERP MEANT

As the discussion moved forward into the ERP world, another dynamic was
added that was not part of the equation when all of the systems used were
"legacy" and homegrown. Now, with commercial, off-the shelf (COTS) applications platforms, additional considerations have to be incorporated into IT
strategy decisions. All of the COTS vendors have a sales model that includes the
initial costs of buying licenses and ongoing maintenance fees for which a
business receives problem-resolution support, updates to existing releases, and
periodic upgrades to new versions that provide an ever-expanding catalogue of
new functionality. We have observed a variety of responses to this new
dynamic, but more important, we have also observed how dramatically this
arrangement can influence the way IT strategy affects how a business operates, the costs to the business that may be viewed as out of its control, and how
different approaches to strategy can have dramatically different positive or
negative impacts on business results. The incorporation of these factors into
IT strategy is a key to the ability of a business to get benefits from new integrated systems. It does, however, call for a new thought process.

The most prevalent approach to developing and managing IT strategy in
support of the ERP environment has been to delay upgrading to new releases
as long as possible, even to the point of upgrading only when the release being
used is about to go out of maintenance (a phenomenon in which the vendor
increases yearly maintenance fees for continued support). There are sometimes valid business reasons for this, such as the existence of numbers of
modifications that make upgrades more difficult and expensive, but several
things may happen when this strategy is adopted. Furthermore, as long as
the upgrade itself is viewed as an unfortunate cost to the business with
no short-term tangible results, why would a business leadership team be
enthusiastic to do it?

In addition, the team is often still struggling to gain benefits from work
already completed. It is not difficult to imagine why this would create strong
resistance to upgrades. Each major upgrade also typically contains thousands
of new enhancements, additional technology, new functions, and resolutions
to the many problems that may exist but probably have not affected any

individual client. These upgrades may make significant-enough changes from previous versions that they require redesigning already-implemented business processes that are working properly. It is easy to see why an organization would see this event as one more beyond its control, one that adds significant cost to the organization and with no perceived benefits. Although it is no wonder that there is no enthusiasm for many of these upgrades, pushing them off until absolutely necessary has significantly negative side effects:

- Little gets done, other than cosmetic changes between upgrades.
- Work requests for all levels of changes to the system are submitted and catalogued. Within a couple of years, this catalogue represents a backlog of requested changes, much of which will never get done, and no attempt has been made to merge them into logical projects. The final result is the creation of significant frustration within the functional user community.
- Upgrade projects become so tedious, complex, and disruptive that little effort is paid to anything but getting them completed.
- Without a return for the investment, the organization operates on a budget that manages IT costs to the lowest level possible, rather than treating the ERP platform as one of the potentially highest-performing assets of the enterprise.

A BETTER WAY

So, what can be done about this situation? The answer lies in viewing the ERP platform as a high-performing asset that should be leveraged through a continuous improvement program that increases spending on the continued development of functionality, but is based on Return on Investment cases that are believable and routinely achieved (clearly, a different cultural expectation). When this occurs, businesses will start to look at the IT function as a business partner and a dynamic part of business performance. Four changes to the mind-set (contextual) need to be adopted in order to achieve this goal, including

1. Stop viewing ERP as purely a cost center, rather than an asset.
2. View ERP as a tool that is expected to produce continuous business benefits (ROI).
3. Eliminate the "cool tools" approach to technology tools.
4. Flatten the investment curve.

There will be technical components of upgrades that by themselves won't produce measurable benefits; however, if the stream of tasks becomes part of larger projects where there are Return on Investment commitments made to functional changes, the upgraded components become part of the work stream that keeps the technology platform current, while using new functions to improve the business and produce tangible benefits. As discussed in Chapter 4, Return on Investment should be looked at as a potential asset of the business, and the investment that produces tangible results can offset some otherwise necessary costs.

Stop Viewing ERP as Purely a Cost Center, Rather Than an Asset

Organizations are often so intent on reducing costs that they fail to view IT applications as an opportunity to achieve a Return on Investment. There are a number of reasons for this. More reasons exist than the three listed here, but these are typical:

1. Failure of earlier projects to achieve predicted results. Often this can be attributed to failure to properly establish a base case, which can be described as the Christopher Columbus School of Management; that is, Columbus left on a journey, didn't know where he was going, got there and didn't know where he was, returned and didn't know where he had been.
2. Failure to consider other, established programs that are based on the same savings. In other words, you can't pick low-hanging fruit if you have already eaten it.
3. Not having established measurement systems that can transcend time to provide accurate accounting.

Based on the evolution of IT during the last two decades, organizations often fail to understand differences between IT operations (where data centers may be able to operate more cost effectively) and IT applications (where the applications define and support business processes that determine business results). If an organization views IT applications as the underlying technology that enables and institutionalizes business processes, then a natural conclusion ought to be that the business and IT functions should operate in a strategic relationship, where business opportunities are identified and IT solutions are developed. All are measured by business contribution—to reduce the cost of operations, to increase revenue, and/or to improve corporate governance (cost avoidance). This requires the IT community to learn more about how its applications drive business results and it requires the business community to understand its responsibility for the definition and execution of its business processes. IT may "own" the applications platform, but the business surely must own its business processes and the results.

If all of this is adopted, IT investments can be managed on a Return on Investment basis, which doesn't mean every dollar spent is recovered, but that the organization has adopted the premise that IT applications costs will be included in other improvement initiatives as a partner and the business held accountable for the results. This changes the traditional thought process used in the past, and without adopting a new approach to setting expectations for IT and its contribution, a business is doomed to repeat history.

View SAP as a Tool That Is Expected to Produce Continuous Business Benefits—ROI

When IT is viewed as an unfortunate cost to the organization, measures are created to avoid as much of this cost for as long as possible. Upgrades are done on an infrequent basis and then often done as "get it in" projects that are rarely based on Return on Investment or designed to use newer application versions productively. Upgrades are often intended simply to avoid increased maintenance costs as older software versions become obsolete. Many times, this practice is seen as a necessity, due to heavy modifications that have been done in earlier projects. This solution creates ongoing costs until these costs are removed and replaced by other approaches (conversion to native SAP business processes, or using services oriented architecture to integrate with proprietary software development). In either case, elimination of modification costs that simply won't disappear should always be considered, in order to reduce longer-term support costs by one method or another.

This approach proposes a whole different mind-set that is more appropriate for the technology age we live in. Going back to Dr. Deming and even earlier, organizations have identified areas where opportunities for improvement may exist, including costs such as inventory or purchase prices or revenue such as back-order reduction to improve market perception and a myriad of others.[1] Organizations that have identified these tend to be healthy organizations that understand that their ability to significantly change their business results must be accomplished by changing business processes.

Because IT applications define business processes at the transaction level, as well as across functions, and then define what data are captured to support analytics and reporting, the IT function must be part of all of these improvement programs. As projects are identified and defined, the use of ERP to enable these improvements can be incorporated into business planning, and all of the potential benefits can be used to justify and pay for the projects. The next step, then, is to flatten the IT investment curve to make these continuing investments part of operating the day-to-day business and avoiding the larger, periodic programs that inevitably become so complex that the return is lost in the rush to get it done. This cannot be a onetime exercise, an off-site meeting day when everyone goes to the woods for team building and then sings "Kumbaya." It is hard work that requires understanding and support from the whole leadership team. Change needs to become a natural part of everyday business planning. It is simply unrealistic to believe that with the constant change in our personal and business environments, an organization can take breaks between change events. If the business can adapt the planning approach to include the constant changes in markets, customers, products, and corporate structure (acquisitions and divestitures, for example), then change can be looked at as opportunity and not as unfortunate events to be overcome.

Eliminate the "Cool Tools" Approach to Technology Tools

The third area is what can be called a "cool tools" approach to the development of IT applications. It is the life mission of ERP vendors to continue to support and develop tools so that organizations can create value from their investments. This does not mean, however, that client organizations should become enamored with all of these tools, except when they make sense and can provide tangible business benefits to the organization. It is necessary to separate business functionality from the marketing hype of vendors, as well as overcome the typical mistrust between business and IT. A consequence of this is that the business organization needs to define more discretely what its true needs are. This comes from

- Understanding current business processes and results.
- Understanding the new or different applications and how these applications can be used to change current conditions.
- Communicating legitimate business needs to the IT community, which must be able to design IT applications and solutions to meet those needs.
- Incorporate new programs and technology into the ongoing project stream that is constantly improving the ability of the overall applications platform to support business needs and produce business benefits.

A good example of this is the area of business reporting in ERP
Internal clients often complain that reporting capability is poor; then IT
a solution to implement a new data warehouse, analytical, or reporting
but IT takes the approach of implementing it and encouraging the u
munity to figure out how to use it. We will grant that providing the
response to the business community expressing frustration with its abili
"reports" out of the application platform; however, when proposed solu
business problems are seen as the responsibility of technologists, soluti
typically be technology based and not specifically targeted to providing
business solutions. In fact, the inability to provide some particular an
report to the business could be buried deeply enough in the design tha
collaborative approach will allow for a solution to be found.

An example is when a sales department may decide it needs
monthly sales not only by sales organization and region but also b
branch. If the configuration of organizational structures has not included the
sales branch as an element, the actual cause of not being able to report by
branch requires changes in the master data for the organizational structures.
Although this is a simplistic example, there are many instances where new
reporting or analytical needs require more than just ad hoc report creation.

A better approach is to figure out exactly what the reporting/analytical
needs are at the business performance level (a business function, not IT)
and, with this functional specification, to allow the IT group to do what it does
best—that is, design a solution to meet a detailed need, using all of the
available tools. Obviously, this will also require the IT support organization to
learn more about how and why certain data elements are configured, created,
collected, and available. This new thought process requires changes in every
function, as the IT support team learns how to actually run the business on
ERP and does not simply try to apply old approaches and attitudes.

As mentioned earlier, this thought process is also promoted by the marketing hype from ERP vendors, but think for a minute about what the vendor
role is in this process. Software companies are in the business of developing
software and selling licenses. That is not startling. In fact, what is startling is
how well they do that in this day of rapidly exploding technologies. We are
now talking about delivering these functions from a "cloud," moving transactions to ad hoc mobility platforms, improving access to data at higher
transaction speeds, and many more. All of these are extremely exciting and all
have important places in tomorrow's technology.

The problem, however, occurs when basic business process issues have
not been resolved, Return on Investment cases have not been built, the real

value to the business of this new technology has not been defined, and, finally, investment decisions have been made on glitzy promises and not on solid business principles. If the problem is in capturing and collating the data, faster, fancier platforms, no matter how modern and fun they are, won't change anything, and we will simply become dissatisfied faster. Worse, when data comes to the field via a salesperson at a client site who can use his or her iPad to create an ad hoc report to get information for a client, we need to consider the knowledge that the salesperson will require in order to ensure that what he or she asks for, creates, and reports to the customer is accurate and reflects the information he or she actually wants to pass on.

Flatten the Investment Curve

What would happen if, instead of major, complex, and expensive "cost of doing business" projects every several years, the business took the same costs, averaged them over the years, and developed a continuous series of projects defined by business needs, based on a Return on Investment and delivered to meet business needs? These projects would be self-funding, from the Return on Investment perspective, and would include all of the technology upgrades necessary to keep up but would be funded by business improvements. This requires thinking of potential Return on Investment, identified and quantified in Chapter 4, as a potential asset of the company that can be spent like any other asset. This program would allow several outcomes:

- Work requests can be evaluated and combined into logical groups as project components, rather than merely seen as costs or, alternatively, can be assessed and addressed in other ways. Every work request that sits in a queue for a year is a reflection of dissatisfaction on somebody's part. Grouping work requests and evaluating them could make that process transparent. Also, work requests placed in queues by different departments are often just different ideas of how to address the same problem and may actually conflict with one another.
- Work requests can be accompanied by clear statements of the value to the organization, both financially and intangibly, a discipline generally included in engineering requests for capital but somehow not required for many IT proposals.
- Projects become less complex, better defined, and more likely to be successful.
- A continuous improvement program governance process can manage this project stream over time.

- New technologies can be employed to meet defined business needs and not just to add glitz to the platform.

EMPOWERING THE FUTURE BY OPTIMIZING THE PAST

All of the discussion in this chapter has focused on changing the collective mind-set of business organizations as they consider the roles that IT and IT strategy play in producing tangible and positive business benefits. There is an old adage that states, "If you can't imagine it, you can't achieve it." This is very true of the potential benefits to be derived from integrated ERP applications. Leaders of business organizations must be able to imagine IT producing positive business benefits continuously over the years. The amount of business returns will, of course, vary from business to business, based on size, on complexity, on the quality of the initial ERP implementation (defined by business process designs), and, always, on the contextual understanding of the relationships among business applications, business processes, and business results. Although this book is focused on using the existing capabilities of these systems and recovering the benefits that have been left on the table, either due to failure to resolve cross-functional design issues or due to functionality not yet implemented, there is another attractive benefit from engaging in this work.

A key to success will depend on how the program governance function discussed in Chapters 10 and 11 is implemented and executed; however, some discussion of governance is warranted here, because the way IT strategy is perceived and defined will either enable or hinder the ability for this business value stream to continue over time. If the program governance function is viewed as one established to manage a continuous improvement program and is a standing function within the business, then it will include a design element that will ensure that the business always looks for future needs and capability that will become available to make the IT applications ever more valuable to the organization. Furthermore, it will incorporate these forward-looking discoveries into the project stream.

So, how might this work? We certainly cannot imagine some of the advances that might be developed during the next 10 years, any more than 10 years ago we could have imagined the proliferation of tools and products that we have today. Let's look at a couple that we can imagine, mostly because they are becoming real as this book is published. The connectivity and speeds that have expanded over the years and certainly show no signs of slowing down will provide exciting opportunities to put more capabilities in the hands of workers faster and in more places than we could have imagined a few years ago. In many practical ways, the real potential is not fully developed yet, but the path forward is very clear. Aside from concerns about social implications of an always-connected workforce or managerial force, the ability to respond to immediate needs, whether on the shop floor, in staff meetings, or in front of clients, is expanding and will only continue. These technologies need to be included in IT strategy considerations, to understand both in the context of your business needs and more broadly.

It is important that clear responsibilities exists to stay connected with these as they develop, to evaluate how they might be deployed to support your business and help you remain close to your customers' needs, and, equally important, to see how they fit into your investment stream and to ensure that they are both deployed as they become available, if the business case warrants it, and that they are all justified, based on clear Return on Investment cases, either by themselves or as part of the larger project stream. We will discuss this much more in Chapters 10 and 11 and then again in the Postscript. For the purpose of this chapter, however, there is a key point to be made here. All of these technology advancements work only if the fundamental task of designing and implementing optimized business processes either has been done or continues to be done. It is critical that while looking to the future, a business team must also look to the present (and perhaps the past, but in a proactive sense, for opportunity, not excuses) and ensure that the hard work of building the business processes that will bring about the lowest costs and the highest performance to the customer have been or are in the process of being implemented. Anything else will simply risk exposing your weaknesses to your customers, faster and in more detail.

All businesses must be in the process of becoming what they will be tomorrow, or they risk continuing to be what they were yesterday, while their competitors build their tomorrows.

SUMMARY

There is an opportunity to stop legitimizing the dichotomy between IT and business leaders and to develop partnerships that will allow for flatter investment curves, with much more of the investment based on detailed ROI, where current conditions, means of measurement, and setting of expectations become the norm. The challenge is to stop treating IT applications like some mysterious life form that has descended on us and to start treating IT applications like all of the other tools that we use to design and operate the enterprise. This will require not only a different mind-set on the part of business leaders but also a different level of understanding among the mid-levels of management in organizations. How a company addresses the need for more education across functions and how it creates a continuous learning environment (discussed in the next chapter) is not as important as is the requirement that the company address this issue, however it must be done. The world we live in and lead businesses in has changed beyond our imagination during the last 25 years, and our ability to keep up has been challenged for sure.

A typical first user experience on a desktop computer in a business occurred about 1984 at the earliest, and most business leaders grew up in a world without this technology. It was years before the use of personal computers became pervasive in the office, longer yet on the manufacturing work floor, and again longer before we got to the point of carrying laptops wherever we went and connecting wirelessly. We have, however, gotten to this point during the last couple of decades, and we cannot imagine a workplace without these tools. Unfortunately, the same relationship with business applications that we use to organize and manage complex business organizations has not kept up. It is the same idea, just much broader, but also much more powerful to derive business benefits. As with every change in our history, it requires a change in our thinking, a change in our behaviors, and a change in the way we relate to coworkers and leadership teams. IT strategy is a large part of supporting this transformation in our thinking but will only occur by acknowledging it and designing a path forward, based on creating business value and not simply on managing costs.

 NOTE

1. W. Edwards Deming, *Out of the Crisis* (Cambridge: Massachusetts Institute of Technology, Center for Advanced Engineering Study, 1982, 1986).

CHAPTER EIGHT

Workforce Education and Readiness

"The tools and ideas presented in this book are for destroying the illusion that the world is created of separate, unrelated forces. When we give up this illusion—we can then build "learning organizations," organizations where people continually expand their capacity to create the results they truly desire, where new and expansive patterns of thinking are nurtured, where collective aspiration is set free, and where people are continually learning how to learn together."

—*Peter Senge,* The Fifth Discipline

 INTRODUCTION

Peter Senge, in his book *The Fifth Discipline*, presents the argument for the creation of a "Learning Organization," an organizational extension of a personal habit of lifelong learning. Although one could argue that the need to continue to learn about the world around you has been important throughout our lifetimes, it is also pretty obvious that we have experienced a period of acceleration in what we need to know to effectively run a business (or even to lead our own lives). It is certainly no surprise that this change calls for broader education and experience in a variety of disciplines for leaders; however, there is little evidence that this has been baked into business models in a post-functional business world.

THE WORKFORCE AS A LEARNING ORGANIZATION

Senior leadership positions play important roles in organizations and have to create a balance in skills and assignments such that all crucial competencies are covered. As we move fully into an integrated business environment, one of the skills areas that must be staffed and led properly is the subject of this book. The sensitivity and attention to this critical aspect of business leadership must be included in the traits of key leaders. We know that personnel are staffed in an organization to help the executive team make decisions that leverage the power of these tools to produce business results. It appears as though this is already being done, but evidence that it is done effectively is difficult to find.

Getting back to my personal story from the Preface for a minute, I was introduced to my first computer (other than gaming systems) in about 1984, when I was 40 years old. My manufacturing plant had acquired an Apple III and placed it in the accounting department, where it sat and gathered dust. Actually, what was lacking was the ability to conceptualize how one might use this new tool in order to produce something of value, often a problem that still exists today in the "cool tools" approach covered in Chapter 7. The two software packages I remember that came with the new computer were PFS (Personal Filing System) and VisiCalc (an early spreadsheet program).

My immediate need was to track absenteeism and tardiness in my workforce of about 80 workers, which was running more than 8 percent and creating problems with scheduling, as well as unhappiness in the workforce among people who had to cover for the offenders. It was simple, really. I needed to record every instance of noncompliance, collate the information by worker, and produce a report that would allow me to identify conclusively the worst offending employees. (Can you imagine? Today we would do this over lunch.) I had been doing that manually, but it was difficult to wade through all of the paperwork and come up with the right answer. PFS allowed me to create a simple four-line form that my supervisors would fill out. On

Fridays, I would enter the information from the forms into the computer, collate the data, and finally report on them. The weekly report that I produced allowed me to sit down with each of the worst offenders and address their issues.

Within a couple of months, the 8 percent became less than 1 percent, which allowed me to introduce a new "replacement worker" policy that significantly changed the way the plant operated. The creation of the report transformed this aspect of operating the plant. Now, I recognize that this is a real "ho-hummer" of a story, considering what we do with computers today, but remember that as a business executive, I had never seen anything like this Apple III computer. The issue was not to learn how to create, collate, or report. The issue was how to conceptualize what could be done with this new tool, much the same as the way business executives are confronted with problems today, on a much larger scale.

My second example presented more of a challenge but was essentially the same issue—not the ability to learn how to use the tool but knowing how to conceptualize what could be done. This theme will carry through this entire discussion about the explosion of technology and capability that continues today, nearly three decades after my first encounter. We were just entering our financial planning and budgeting season for the following year. Our plant had four lines of product, all of which were processed through the same equipment in campaigns and each of which operated at different speeds. Given the difference in processing speeds, the product mix was obviously a large component of calculating product costs, staffing, and capacity.

The way our budget process worked was that a proposed product mix would be developed by division headquarters (several hundred miles away), then phoned to me, and we would massage the numbers, formulate a rough production plan, add the staffing and other costs, and call it back to headquarters. Typically, this would take a couple of days. Because I was "playing" with the new computer, I created a simple spreadsheet program (today the complexity of it would be laughable) that had product on one axis and demand on the other. Calculation of production time requirements was created by using simple math and cascaded "if" functions, because look-up tables came much later (or I simply didn't find them). Once my spreadsheet was complete, I simply typed in the product mix and called the answer back to headquarters. Inevitably, this was followed by a second version of demand, but now, instead of another day or more, the results were returned in a few minutes. After several iterations of demand and exhortations to "take these seriously," which were based on the expectation that it would take days, our controller and IT director actually got on an airplane and flew to the plant to see for themselves how I was doing this.

A couple of points in this story are valuable to this discussion. The first is that neither the controller nor the IT director could conceive how this analysis could be produced without either lengthy calculation or some sort of mainframe programming that only headquarters had access to. Far from being a story of bad leaders, this is a story of the start of our current technology and points out that none of us in my generation (who are in senior leadership positions today) grew up with computers, knew how they would operate, or were aware of how they might be employed to accomplish important work. In 1983, we were all learning together. There are two additional points to make here. A couple of years ago, my four-year-old grandson was "playing" with his mother's laptop on the kitchen table and after a while asked his mother for her credit card number, obviously raising concerns. It turns out that he had turned on the computer, opened the browser, navigated to MLB.com, filled his shopping basket with baseball paraphernalia, and proceeded to the checkout screen. For him, this was intuitive at the age of four. The ability to employ these technology tools becomes easier and easier for individuals as our workforce becomes more and more populated with people who grew up with technology.

The second point is that we simply cannot keep up with the potential of these tools unless we commit ourselves to lives of continuous learning about how these tools work and how we can apply them. Furthermore, this requires being able to conceptualize how to use these tools, as well as cultivating the technical skills to effectively use them. The same applies to organizations, where the competence of businesses to apply these tools will continue to be a product of the collective knowledge of the workforce, from executives to line workers.

Here is another example that will seem laughable to most of today's generation. In the earliest days of Internet e-mail communications (in this case, mainframe based), I would send an e-mail message to my director in Germany and then call his admin to let her know that I had sent it. She would open his e-mail account, print out the note, put it on his desk, get his written response, type it back into his e-mail, and send it to me. He was determined to be seen as current and forward-thinking and so was sensitive enough to at least create the perception of adopting new technology. Today that same executive gets my e-mail on his smartphone during lunch and replies immediately. Learning how to effectively use technology has become easier but

requires a constant learning environment, both individually and collectively. As one gets into the world of ERP, many things change and become more complex, but many things also remain the same, and the solutions still rest on basic skills, understanding, and the ability to conceptualize how these tools can be deployed to produce business benefits.

In another example taken from 1995, I had a division that had just implemented an ERP package across multiple manufacturing plants, as well as headquarters. The general manager asked me to his office and announced to me that the ERP system didn't work. On my asking what his immediate concern was, he responded that he could not see the raw material inventory at one of his plants. I asked him to log on to his system so that I could help him see the inventory, which obviously could be seen—and I got a blank stare. He then called his administrative assistant and asked her whether she could remember the log-on ID and password, and she gave them to me. Once in the system, I was able to look at the inventory location in question and see that it showed no inventory of the material in stock; however, the plant had reported that the location was, in fact, full. The VP GM came to the conclusion that the ERP program didn't work—rather than arriving at the obvious understanding (looking back) that for some reason the receipts had never been entered in the system. My point here is not to disparage the VP GM, who had only recently learned to do e-mail on his computer (remember, this was 1995), and he wasn't proficient at typing, either, which made him even more uncomfortable on the computer. My point is that today's generation of leaders did not grow up with these systems and have had to learn during the last couple of decades to conceptualize better how these systems work and how they can be used. In many cases, this generation of leaders feels overwhelmed when implementations or upgrades of highly complex ERP applications take longer, cost more, and sometimes deliver less.

 ## WORKFORCE EDUCATION

We have introduced through personal examples the need to engage in an educational program throughout a working lifetime, so that we can continue to learn about both the ERP systems that are being used and the business processes that determine business results; now let's take a closer look at the components of education that are needed. We need to address what is needed in an enterprise, in training and education, to allow a business to make the most effective use of this extraordinarily expensive and powerful asset in the following areas:

- Transactional training
- Functional or technical training
- Business education in an integrated business world

Transactional Training

Although this level of training seems intuitively obvious, in real-life execution, it can be anything but. There are many instances of remediation activities at companies that were close to having to shut down because of inadequate or, in certain instances, a complete lack of initial training. In these cases, the consulting organizations that were responsible typically recommended a training approach for the workforce that was deemed "too expensive," and consequently initial training was nothing more than "point and click." Sometimes, the costs for that decision were nearly detrimental to the business.

As ERP business processes are designed and configured, many decisions have to be made on business processes, on organizational levels, and on how the required information is going to be collected. This latter level requires that individual fields on input screens be defined, the data being either required or optional, and how the fields are populated has to be determined (from master data or from the operator, for example). Also, the design decisions reflect how these transactions will affect how the business is intended to operate, as well as affect the results expected.

As a simple example, in a standard cost system for materials, standard cost is determined and entered into a master data file and then the cost on the line-item level of the purchase order is automatically entered by the transaction. For nonstandard items (noninventory, for example), there are options on how this is done, and it reflects a business rule decided on by the company. As each transaction is designed, information around how the transaction works is collected at the screen field level; it is important that this information become part of an educational program for the people eventually assigned responsibility for these data. You can imagine that in many organizations, this knowledge is passed on by "word of mouth" or by "on the job training" by the workers. This may work well in a business environment where work is assigned at this job level (it probably doesn't, but I'm giving the benefit of the doubt). Yet this may not work well in an integrated ERP environment, where the more that individual workers understand, the better the performance of the system.

In addition, there is always turnover or expansion, and there may or may not be formal planning for ongoing education. Just as in the old story of sitting around a campfire and one person starts to tell a story to the person next to him, who then in turn reports it to the next person, and around the campfire until it returns to the original teller, the same invariably happens with on-the-job training programs that are not formal and structured—the training at the end of the line is not what was intended at the start.

Another aspect is that nothing in the world we live in is static, and it is unreasonable to expect our business world to be any different. The ERP system will have to evolve to keep up as a business changes. This can be on a macro basis, where there may be acquisitions or divestitures, or it can be simple and at the departmental level. An example is where one of the sales personnel signs an agreement to provide a consigned stock inventory location at the customer's plant.

Obviously, the ERP system will have to be changed to accommodate this and, depending on business rules, could involve the use of new plant codes, inventory locations, stock types, goods movement types, and more. If these changes are not incorporated into documentation that is used for training pur- poses and the changes explained to the workforce, new or transferred employees will not have access to "as built" records for the systems they will be using, and knowledge of how these systems operate will slowly but inevitably decline.

Here is another real-life example. During the design of master data records for materials, a field was enabled in the accounting data where the line of business that the material (in this case, finished goods) belonged to was indi- cated. Also, the material master was created by several different departments, rather than being a centralized function, and the proposed master record creation was managed using workflow, which is typically a good way to manage this process. The problem, however, was that the design team could not get the accounting department to agree that this field should be "required," and, con- sequently, it was left "optional" during creation. Although there may have been some logic for this decision, it became a serious issue after implementation. The business had a legacy data warehouse system that produced reports that were used by the four lines of business and produced end-of-period financial reports. This report collated sales transactions from this optional field when the trans- action data were moved from the ERP platform into the data warehouse. Because a significant number of sales materials records had a blank in this box, a rule was established that the lack of an entry would be interpreted as belonging to the largest of the four lines of business.

Politically, the best that could be determined was that this empty-entry solution was done as a default because there was still not agreement on who would complete this field and how. This meant that the sales for the largest product line were significantly inflated and that the sales for each of the others were understated. It took weeks to find the problem within the data warehouse, even though the answer was pretty intuitive in hindsight. The people who designed the data warehouse very likely never knew what problem they created, and the implementation team had moved on without adequately training the workforce.

This issue could have been resolved either by the data warehouse designers forcing a decision on how blank fields would be interpreted, by making the field "required" (which was ultimately done), or by training the workers in the accounting department on the importance of this selection and how to make the determination—essentially, a transaction training issue. Furthermore, it is likely that there was a transition of programmers or assignments that resulted in the knowledge of the warehouse design not being passed on.

Functional or Technical Training

Beyond the transactional level, each functional area within the company needs to have expertise in how its entire function operates and what the potential associated with different processes might be, so that business issues that arise can be analyzed and reasonable cross-functional business process changes can be proposed, reviewed, and agreed on. In order to do this, an organization needs to ensure that there is sufficient functional knowledge, either within the department itself or within the IT support function for departments, to understand potential solutions. The purpose of this section refers to the need to fully understand each function and what the capabilities of the applications package are for all of them. These resources can then engage across functional boundaries to other stakeholders, assuming that this conversation is part of the organizational culture. If this is not done and maintained, reasonably simple business problems can quickly escalate into blaming the ERP system for preventing the resolution of issues, rather than seeing it as a powerful tool to support change.

Typically, functional project team members are selected to attend one or more additional functional training courses at academies or through on-site programs that can be tailored to the individual enterprise if there are sufficient student candidates. The problem with the last approach is that one wants the super users or experts to know more about the available functionality than simply understanding what has been done. This is to prepare those super users or experts for future development needs or for the possible resolution of current problems. The broader scope of knowledge that is designed into standard academy courses is valuable to create knowledge of potential solutions in functional experts. Of course, the enthusiasm for "new" things needs to be managed by the permanent governance process that will be the subject of Part III of this book.

In addition, this skill set should be one of continuing education, both through ERP training and also through participation in various industry councils, such as user groups supported by the software companies, where different approaches are discussed. Just as in seminars designed to increase employee knowledge of functional areas or company programs that are part of continuing education, constantly improving ERP knowledge is essential for an organization to move toward a true learning environment. One point, however, bears repeating.

There is also a difference between various training programs that create understanding, both at a conceptual and at a transactional level, of how the system does or could operate and similar programs that are designed to sell the future. Future development opportunities are interesting and perhaps valuable; however, this section deals with the current and evolving everyday needs of the business. It is often difficult to separate the two, yet these are really two very different uses for the training venues, and both in their right times are important. You will see in Chapter 10 that controlling the relationship between these two needs may be done through a program governance process that should be established to manage business changes over time. To put it another way, it is important to recognize and respect the following two aspects of this:

1. As the ERP platform and functionality improve and expand over time, it is necessary to have established programs to allow functional super users to keep up with the possibilities. It is simply more difficult to conceptualize how these new capabilities can produce business benefits if you are unaware of the potential and what these capabilities have been created to address.
2. All software vendors are in the business of creating software with functionality that can produce tangible business benefits for a client. They are also in the business of using this development to sell additional licenses, either through expanding the number of users or by creating further

acceptance of their applications. This does not mean, however, that new capabilities are aligned with business needs immediately or that they shouldn't wait to be planned into the long-term continuous improvement programs to create additional business value. This whole process must be managed and evaluated in order for workers to avoid becoming enamored with technology that is too advanced for a company's current situation, despite how valuable it may be at the right time.

BUSINESS EDUCATION IN AN INTEGRATED BUSINESS WORLD

We have covered the most obvious training and education needs, but perhaps the most important (for long-term business health) is typically not even considered. As cross-functional business process understanding has been developed during the last 50 years or more, knowledge of how it works was held in the hands of a trusted few, later disseminated to a few more, and eventually communicated to much larger constituency groups but always within artificial boundaries. This is true of such programs as MRP I, MRP II, and Project Management, as well as the design capabilities of modern ERP systems. In both of the earlier cases, certification programs were developed by industry groups such as APICS (American Production and Inventory Control Society) and PMI (Project Management Institute), and large numbers of people were encouraged to take these programs to become certified. In fact, this includes a much larger number than ever who became practitioners of the particular skill sets. Understanding these concepts and how they apply to business design and execution became components of ongoing individual learning programs to develop these advanced skill sets. ERP programs tend to be much broader than either of the aforementioned and have progressed more slowly as part of general educational awareness in industry. Yet the time to address these needs becomes more apparent every day, as businesses get past managing ERP as a cost center and an administrative tool and start to look at ERP as an effective tool to derive business results.

The ability to envision how this works, however, is much more complex than simply an IT process, and it must be incorporated into the educational programs that work on continually improving overall workforce readiness. In order to truly derive business benefits from ERP investments, an enterprise will have to undertake a program to reverse this pattern and provide opportunities to continually gain deeper understanding of the potential benefits available through the use of ERP applications. This is not to compete with the IT department but to help in understanding how the business operates and why. After all, this is a business function supported by IT applications; it is not IT technology inflicted on business owners. There are limited certification programs provided by vendors—for example, SAP has a program that addresses this need: TERP 10 Business Process Integration Certification. This program defines all of the business processes that exist in its ERP business suite products and provides a cross-functional view of how and why ERP relationships determine to a great degree how business benefits are derived in its product. Other vendors also have similar programs, or they can be created.

In addition, there are university programs that include courses on business process integration and a variety of other courses that can help with this educational need. These and other programs can be included in individual learning plans developed to promote personal growth. However, universities have been slow to develop programs in ERP applications that have become ubiquitous in industry, and more should be encouraged to produce undergraduate and graduate courses and programs to address this need.

Reasons for this slow program development may reflect the attitudes of leaders or faculty at university programs, because they typically don't want to teach "products" or they consider this effort to be training, which is often viewed as more of a tech school skill set. These perceptions could not be further from the truth. Understanding how these properly developed educational/academic programs deliver instructional materials/courses that teach about the way in which the integrated business world operates is a true educational achievement and not an example of pure skills training. It is more along the lines of why we study business strategy in M.B.A. programs and deserves to be approached with the same academic rigor as those subject areas. We need to promote a paradigm shift in cognitive understanding, such that other skills training programs can be better understood in the context of cross-functional business processes.

A short discussion of the differences between undergraduate and graduate business education is useful here. A dichotomy that is both simplistic and somewhat arbitrary but will help differentiate them follows. The distinction presented here in relation to the subject of this book is valuable. An undergraduate is gaining an understanding of basic competencies or skill sets in independent subject areas. Accounting, strategy, financial analysis, economic principles, logistics, perhaps IT applications, and others are subjects where the expected learning outcomes are pretty well limited to the subject of each individual course. It is typically left to students to figure out how these relate to one another, in many cases. Graduate programs, however, are strongest when they not only teach more depth in individual subject areas but also teach the relationships between functions and how all of that relates to business outcomes. This is one reason that the use of broad case studies has grown over the years and is particularly true when teaching M.B.A. students how to use ERP applications to produce business results. It is a case of learning the "what" in undergraduate business programs and learning the "how" and "why" in graduate programs, and to achieve this, it requires relating individual course materials to one another.

Although there are a large number of schools where some ERP courses are taught, very few have comprehensive programs to teach ERP as a cross-functional business competency. Even fewer attempt to offer a comprehensive program that teaches students how to achieve business benefits using ERP technology. An example of one of these programs is the online ERP Graduate Certificate Program that is part of the M.B.A. curriculum at Central Michigan University. As more companies seek this kind of educational program, other universities will be encouraged to further develop this important business school curriculum.

This interrelating or integrating of individual course materials to one another is important even if we are not talking about graduate programs. It is a challenge to universities and businesses, both of which have been designed around a functionally organized world, not the integrated business process world that we live in. For businesses, it may seem impossible to find appropriate educational opportunities to use with the workforce; however, success still rests on the ability of leadership and management ranks to acquire this understanding. For universities, it is also a challenge to business school leadership and faculty to develop broader knowledge of the relationship between functions, rather than simply the internal workings of a unit or a discipline.

As an example, take a course in financial responsibility. Although it is easy to conceive how this topic would include working with regulatory standards and auditing approaches, it is also crucial that it include knowledge of where in the organization internal controls issues arise and where they need to be addressed. It is difficult to audit a process by looking only at the results. Knowledge of sources is becoming more necessary as integrated business processes become more complex. Only through the process of broadening the syllabi for these courses will we start to really teach students how the integrated business world operates and how to lead and manage in that environment.

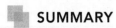 **SUMMARY**

The transition to an ERP environment involves more than just work process decisions and technical configuration. It also requires an organization to take a broader, longer-term, and more detailed look at how to create a permanent program to promote the development of a true learning environment. This need must be detailed at the transaction level, as well as at the expert level, where functional knowledge is based. The organization must include the use of higher education to continue to increase understanding in its business leaders, from managers to executives (including those who aspire to be part of this group). Initially, participation in business process integration education (possibly to include certification simply as confirmation of achieving the goals) was a good start in the development of a cadre of individuals in the organization who could discuss business performance issues in terms of the underlying support systems. Now, this role is no longer deferred to technical teams, and it provides the opportunity to create business partnerships between business and IT.

After initial cross-functional business process training, continued entrenchment of this understanding can be pursued through the support of individual university programs. Just as with the introduction of other technologies and approaches over the years, achieving an understanding of how to harness the power of ERP systems to gain maximum benefits requires a lifetime commitment to organizational and personal education programs. The dynamic here is the collective knowledge in the workforce of cross-functional process relationships (the how and the why, not only the what) that allows for a discussion of design points between departments based on the greatest total value for the organization as a whole.

One final word and an example are illustrative of current narrow-minded approaches. On a number of occasions while performing audits of ERP programs, either during implementation or afterward, we encountered parts of the organization that clearly, and with the admission of the client, did not have sufficient, let alone optimal, knowledge of their areas of responsibility in the new application. When we pointed this out to the leaders of the client organization, a typical response was that they knew it; however, they were afraid that if they sent certain employees to training programs to develop their knowledge and skills in order to perform their functions properly, the employer would not be able to retain these employees in the organization.

This approach, therefore, hogties the organization to suboptimal performance, rather than addressing the retention issues by other means. Though, admittedly, this can be an issue, an organization suffers significantly greater loss of profitability by limiting the collective knowledge of the organization than it would suffer by adopting any other approach. It all goes back to Peter Senge. It is simply necessary in our rapidly expanding world of technology and analytical tools to adopt the philosophy of the Learning Organization and develop the means to ensure that the collective knowledge of the organization is constantly growing to meet its needs.

How this is accomplished must be incorporated into the long-term view of how the organization designs, implements, and uses these ERP applications. All of this needs to be a component of the continuous improvement process, which will be discussed in Part III.

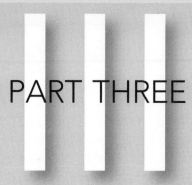

PART THREE

A New Program Governance Approach

P ART III focuses on developing and implementing an action plan to enable a business to take the output from the analyses and incorporate it into a continuous improvement plan that will be sustaining over time and keep the organization focused on achieving a Return on Investment. The five analyses are used to construct a program governance approach focused on leading the organization through change processes at all levels of the business.

- Chapter 9, "Integration of Organizational Needs": This chapter will discuss the process of integrating all of the data collected during the preparation phase in Part II. It will present organizational issues and concepts to deal with the integration of cross-functional and cross-leader issues to produce a single comprehensive path forward.
- Chapter 10, "Developing a Governance Process": Throughout this book, as we have created a new understanding of organizational issues and challenges, we have referred to the need for a more comprehensive program governance function to manage the process of business transformation. In Chapter 10, we propose a tiered program to address these needs.
- Chapter 11, "Organizational Change Management": As pointed out throughout this book, success or failure ultimately is determined by the

ability of the project teams to deal with organizational change issues, both with workers who will be affected by the changes and also with executives whose compensation and careers may be affected. This chapter proposes a new way to deal with these issues.

- Chapter 12, "Conclusions and Opportunities": We have created a new view of leadership's role in achieving business benefits, have taken new contextual views of the business, merged the discoveries into a single comprehensive program, and established a governance program to keep us on track and an organizational change management function to deal with change. Chapter 12 looks at where we are ready to go in the future with our newfound success.

Integration of Organizational Needs

"I have selected these three activities not only because they are of major concern in most organizations but also because they illustrate several important puzzles. The four puzzles are that (1) the activities that produce success also produce failure; (2) how the success is framed covers up the failure; (3) the criteria of success in all three cases are not tough enough to deal with the problems that plague managers at all levels in many different kinds of organizations; and (4) in all cases, the players involved are not getting at the basic causes of the problems. They are solving problems in superficial ways, and they are unrealizingly kidding themselves that this is not so."

—*Chris Argyris*, Overcoming Organizational Defenses

INTRODUCTION

Just as we have taken a process view of each of the following five aspects of business and suggested new ways of looking at each one, we now need to take a process view of how they all fit together. Before we can put an effective governance process in place to oversee the program (the immediate program, as well as the long-term stream of projects that will/should occur), we need to evaluate the output from the analyses conducted in Part II as a group:

- Return on Investment
- Business process management
- Cultural/political/organizational analysis
- IT strategy
- Workforce readiness

This discussion requires a balanced approach to setting the goals and direction of the enterprise and must include an appreciation for issues that have to be addressed by the leadership team. If you accept the premise that viewing the business from traditional perspectives has failed to produce optimum business results, then the idea that a new cognitive and analytical approach to understanding complex business issues can produce different results should be obvious. It will make no difference how business process designs will be achieved if there is no agreement on how to analyze and design across functions. Furthermore, it is necessary to have the understanding that those difficult issues directly, and possibly adversely, affecting department executives will be addressed within this process.

For example, it will make no difference how the Return on Investment process is constructed and managed if the IT strategy around upgrades, new modules, or resolution of "work orders" by functions is not incorporated into the mix. This balanced approach will identify and address many similar issues that may challenge conventional management approaches.

Throughout this process, IT leaders must be fully engaged on technical issues, where they will be looked to for their technical knowledge and skills. In addition, they need to be involved in business issues, which will have a direct impact on how the new IT functionality will be deployed, managed, and supported. It is also important to note that every effort must be made to approach this with a team of workers who

- Have the full support of their functional and senior leaders. There is often a tendency to relegate these assignments to anyone who is available. If this person also happens to be a respected leader in his or her function, this is fine; however, when that is not the case, adjustments need to be made to make the correct individual available.
- Are in a small enough group to be workable and a large enough one to represent all stakeholders. This is highly dependent on the size and complexity of the organization and the scope of the proposed program. A team of 20 is likely too many, because discussions will be difficult to conclude, while a team of 3 probably won't cover enough territory. The answer will vary from one organization to another.
- Are knowledgeable about the organization and leadership such that the output of these studies will make sense to them. This is really calling on their knowledge of the organization, which is likely not sufficient in a junior person, no matter how bright. These designs are going to have to be explained to senior leaders, so knowledge of the organization is crucial.
- Are good at collaborative discussion and decision making. These are two different skills. Often people are good at discussing but timid at making decisions, while others may want to make decisions before fully understanding the issues. Finding representatives with both of these key skills is necessary.
- Are willing to take on "sacred cows," when necessary, to develop a program for long-term continuous improvement. Though I'm not suggesting that the members of this group should be kamikaze, the courage and respect in the organization to describe things as they are is very important.
- Will include an experienced facilitator who can keep the focus aligned with the objectives. This is a highly political process and needs a confident, inclusive but determined leader.

Without a group that has these characteristics, this process can easily become just another exercise in futility. Remember that previously, the organization may have left these issues not clearly identified, and the organization may also have expected them to be resolved by the project teams it empowered to design and implement the new business processes. Also, in many cases, the project team may not be able to resolve issues effectively, resulting in overruns, failures, and, at the very least, reduced realized Return on Investment.

Although a stepwise approach on how to manage this process will be presented here, we recognize that every situation, every company, and every design will follow a different path. The points to be made here are meant to be directional, and the actual design of the implementation plan must be determined by the participants. However, the fundamental principles for how this team should be built and should work are universal. In this book, we have tried to stay away from rigid formulas, while suggesting possible logical approaches. This process will continue in this section, laying out the issues, suggesting possible approaches, but leaving the final designs to the individual business. The end result will be more a matter of how this gets accomplished, rather than adherence to a specific prescription for organizational transformation.

APPROACH TO THE ANALYSIS PROCESS

As a starting point, during the study, each of the analysis teams must compile a list of insights and/or decisions that have been made or recommended. These should, as much as possible, be expressed in clear terms such that the discovery and the effects are understood by the group. The entire group should first review these and agree that they are valid observations or modify them so that agreement is achieved.

It is worth noting that if the group decides to make any significant modifications to the observations/recommendations, these modifications/recommendations should be discussed with the original study group to ensure that any strong arguments for or against the changes are considered. As a comprehensive program is developed, it makes no sense that basic issues remain contentious at this point. Discussion points must include

1. **A complete list of all recognized potential for Return on Investment.** This includes the obvious cost areas, such as materials (inventory), manufacturing parameters (capacity, yield, and accuracy), headcount (both line workers and management), contract costs, and others. It should also include revenue-enhancing areas, such as increased sales, reduced returns, new products, and so on. Although costs are more easily quantified, it is also necessary to create estimates of contributions to profitability based on revenue-increasing actions. It is important that the study group include someone (or more than one person) who understands cost structures and margins so that these can be expressed as increased profits. The point is, some increased sales may produce greater margins than others, and increased volume may not always be a good thing.

   We experienced an example of this some years ago, where the highest-volume product in the plant actually did not fully recover the total costs to manufacture (however, it did recover variable costs). This product was used to base-load manufacturing lines and paid for overhead that was inflexible within the volume range we were experiencing. When sales of this product were expanded, it caused an increase in costs associated with the new production that actually reduced profitability. There is an old adage that goes, "We lose money on every sale, but make it up in volume." Best efforts must be made to quantify in accurate terms what the proposed changes will contribute to overall profitability. This is an important point, because the volume versus overhead consumption for commodity products may be a complicated answer at different manufacturing volumes. The point here is not just for this specific example but to emphasize the need to have members of the team who fully understand these cost functions and their dynamics so that accurate estimates of real financial impact can be obtained. This accuracy is essential to create credibility in the Return on Investment estimates.

2. **Critical process design issues or requirements.** It will be difficult to get consensus later if there is no basic agreement at the start on what the issues are. This can be as simple as deciding what functions are needed to address political challenges, as well as which department will own the decisions. As the earlier study group took a new look at business process management, with the eye to taking a "whole systems" approach to design processes, the study group should have produced recommended methods and tools for use in business process design. This must incorporate existing approaches, knowledge of business process design capabilities in the ERP package, and knowledge of business process management tools and programs, from long-term business process management programs to shorter-term programs used to analyze the current state, identify issues or problems, and design new cross-functional designs to address identified opportunities. The recommendations of the study group, along with detailed rationale for the design, should be discussed and a clear design process adopted for the transformation program.

3. **Characteristics of the current systems that will have either a positive or a negative effect on the integrated process.** Everyone agrees that legacy systems have grown over the years. In some cases, a logical alignment between functions has occurred or programs have been created to keep these systems in general alignment (at times, interfaces that are complex enough to be programs in their own right). A good example is where one inventory system is used to receive and manage inventory, while another one is used to ship the same materials. This challenge may have been addressed by an overnight program where transactions in each

system were performed in the other so that a single version of the truth occurs once each day and then the systems diverge again until the next night. There are times that critical functions within the business are written into interfaces; consequently, it is necessary to understand exactly what the interfaces actually do. For example, if the two operational systems were constructed with different data models, this group can identify the decisions that will have to be made as a single comprehensive configuration is developed. All components of the existing applications landscape must be included, including informal, and perhaps previously unknown to many, programs, to keep them aligned.

4. **Lists of ongoing change/improvement initiatives.** All ongoing change/improvement initiatives will have to either be incorporated into the enterprise change management program or be identified with the relationship between those initiatives and the comprehensive program clearly defined.

Let's look back to the question posed in Part II: "When was the last time that your organization hired a leader with the instructions to change nothing and to operate things exactly as they are?" The corollary of this is that all leaders have plans and objectives to improve the performance of their areas, designed to support corporate needs on which compensation and promotions are dependent. Without incorporating these into the governance program, the organization will always be at odds with itself, and the focus will be on those behaviors that receive the greatest incentives. This is simply a case of how incentive programs create both intended and unintended consequences. This means that the work group must determine for each existing improvement program whether it is going to be

- Part of the overall ERP program;
- Independent of the ERP program because the improvement program neither conflicts with the overall ERP program nor uses resources that will now be managed by the comprehensive governance process; or
- Eliminated or incorporated, because it may be in conflict with or is redundant to elements of the larger program that is being designed.

As part of this discussion process, recommendations for inclusion or elimination must be resolved with current program owners. This is typically not an easy or comfortable discussion; however, if people avoid addressing the fundamental conflict at this point, it just keeps the conflict alive later into the project and often leads to failure. We have found that more often than not, this addresses the basic difference between agreeing to support the new program as part of the staff and not being willing to make the personal changes necessary to allow the program to be effective.

5. **A list of key people in the organization who will be affected by the designs.** The list of key people must include not only the departments that will be affected by the potential changes but also the people in the organization who may feel that their previous contributions are being overlooked. The size of the company working through this process can have an impact on how this proceeds, however, often not in the direction that is commonly thought. There is a general belief that the smaller the company, the easier these decisions become. Yet one of the most difficult implementations we have experienced was in a very small company. Although it had revenue of nearly $200M, most of the revenue was from import/resale. Nearly every business process in the home office had been developed and implemented by the current department leader, who was also a part of the implementation team. Every redesign to accomplish cross-functional integration was seen as a direct criticism of the existing processes. Ownership is something that we strive for as leaders; however, as discussed in Part II, it must also be considered in implementing major changes such as these. It is important to look beyond the obvious, because the designer may have moved on to other functions but may still be invested in the current process.

6. **Identification of destructive incentives and other impediments to accepting changes at all levels of the organization.** We have used this term, *destructive incentives*, to refer to incentives for executives that inadvertently produce competition between departments where logically there must be winners and losers. Because this is often the product of a leadership process that creates a vision, aligns executives to the vision for the company, and has them individually develop objectives to do their part, the issue is with functional alignment within the organization and not with the vision or the programs themselves.

Without fully understanding the cross-functional implications of some objectives, compensation programs are created that motivate them to accomplish individual objectives without ever resolving these implicit conflicts. The problem then occurs when the lack of cross-functional interactions or, worse, the intentional creation of objectives for political advantage become institutionalized into the cultural and political environment. ERP will expose these and other conflicts, which can and must be addressed, either during the project or before the project begins. If some departments already know that other departments have conflicting objectives that have already been established for some misguided or unintentional reason, it is necessary to address these conflicts at this point in developing a new integrated approach to managing the business. This can be embedded deep into the organization.

Some years ago, a program was being developed to use leveraged resources, improving the average experience level of resources and deploying them to meet the needs of customers to reduce their overall costs. The account managers, however, were specifically incentivized to produce increased revenue from their account. This represented a large part of their incentive income. As the intent of the new program was to reduce costs for the client by reducing revenue for the service company, the account management refused to accept the new program. Ultimately, the account was lost, partly because the provider could not demonstrate its ability to help reduce costs. The point is that people will work as they are incentivized to, regardless of larger corporate objectives. If these conflicts cannot be resolved, these destructive incentives may well render this entire process futile. This is why members of the evaluation team must have the confidence and support of senior leadership. It is also one of the primary reasons that the Program Governance Office concept is introduced in the next chapter to help overcome organizational resistance at management levels.

7. **An analysis of current IT strategy.** As the analysis of current IT strategy pertains to continued support for the applications platform, the IT strategy must be clearly defined. It is important to understand the strategy for technical and operational IT processes because these processes may also have a direct or indirect impact on applications strategy. As this process proceeds, IT leadership has the opportunity to become leaders in identifying business process issues, proposing solutions, and leading the organization in designing, implementing, and managing these processes as business partners, as discussed in Chapter 3. The group performing the joint evaluation needs to ensure that the full potential for flattening the investment curve, breaking the projects into smaller, less complex pieces, and justifying each of them with Return on Investment calculations has been completed.

Although this may seem obvious and perhaps unlikely, the following example is all too common and should be avoided. A past company was evaluating its approach to implementing ERP and decided that it would attempt to perform the entire suite implementation at one time. The primary deciding factor was the avoidance of interface development that would be required to divide the project into phases that would then be discarded when the next phase was completed. Total estimates for a temporary interface design was approximately $500,000. The complexity of the project was greater than the organization's ability to keep it on track, because of both weak project controls and extreme complexity, which challenged the business's ability to keep up with the critical path.

Ultimately, the project completion was delayed for six months, costing the company close to $2M in overruns. Now, there is no guarantee that the smaller, shorter, less complex projects would have been successful. However, the cost of failure to stay on the critical path will nearly always result in greater costs than the cost of some temporary interfaces. There is no right answer, but the discussion is valuable to find the least costly path with the higher probability of success.

8. **The effects on the current collective skills inventory.** Specifically, what will be challenging during the proposed programs must be evaluated in light of the total knowledge of the organization. Remember, in a business world that is experiencing or has experienced so much change during the last couple of decades, it is necessary to create a Learning Organization where all employees are encouraged to learn more about process views of the organization, capabilities of the new software, and how to contribute to both the transformation and the future success of the business.

This is the time to create workforce educational strategies that will ensure that the collective knowledge of the workforce will continue to increase. Additionally, it is important that the ability to use that collective knowledge to align corporate processes with customer needs continue, along with the capability to apply this knowledge to continually increase workforce productivity. ERP applications are the programs that can look across traditional boundaries and create the kinds of understanding necessary to smoothly deal with issues that arise. Listing the challenges here will allow for the creation of programs to address this over time and advance the collective knowledge of the business's workforce.

Other than silly examples, it is difficult to see how any kind of business education can do anything but help an organization to improve its ability to detect cross-functional issues and develop solutions. During the integration process, skills deficiencies in the workforce should be identified and addressed. These programs don't necessarily have to be large, because sometimes just getting things started can create knowledge that eventually proves to be useful.

To simplify this discussion, the output from this dialogue must include the following elements:

- Potential Return on Investment opportunities.
- Critical process design issues or requirements.
- Characteristics of the current systems.
- Lists of ongoing change/improvement initiatives.
- List of key people in the organization who will be affected by the designs.
- Identification of destructive incentives and other impediments to accepting changes at all levels of the organization.
- Analysis of current IT strategy.
- Effects on the current collective skills inventory.

 ## CONSOLIDATION

Once the discussion points in the previous section are agreed to, the next step is to evaluate overlap, with particular attention to those areas that have the potential to create a situation where agreement on resolution will be difficult. It often turns out that the issues revolve around competing ideas to resolve conflicts, but the resolution becomes relatively obvious when the issue is clearly defined and discussed.

Remember that ERP platforms are applications that define logical relationships between functions, and, once understood, issues that appeared previously as areas of conflict simply become an opportunity to design a new cross-functional process. One must remember, though, that during these discussions, the members of the design team must remain sensitive to the needs of the functional executives they represent. There will be issues raised where the solution may be obvious, but agreement and implementation may require significant personal changes or sacrifices at the executive level.

This is of crucial importance because there is nothing that will destroy the effectiveness of a program more quickly than a design issue that the project team resolves and then finds a roadblock when it is explained to the team's executive sponsors. We will talk more about how to deal with these issues during the next two chapters on governance and organizational change management in the executive suite. For now, just keep in mind that as these elements and analyses are discussed, it is imperative to identify those issues that will end up being significant roadblocks as the detailed processes are designed later and to open the discussion at this point.

As an example of how issues can be identified at this stage of the design process for the continuous improvement program, let's refer back to the example laid out in Chapter 1. Following the list of information collected, let's assume this scenario:

1. The inability to effectively deal with large global accounts across legal reporting lines is creating significant contractual issues with these clients. In order to better deal with cross-boundary challenges, it is deemed necessary to view staffing and deployment decisions on a global basis. This will require the ability to see staff, revenue, and margins globally.
2. In the current system, resources are assigned to various business lines by the nature of the business being supported; however, many of these resources have broad general skill sets (such as project management) that can be applied across multiple lines of business, and the assignments are made more on the basis of account objectives.
3. There may have been actions taken at account, national, or regional level to address some of these, but they have been ineffective at fully resolving the issue.
4. This affects the net income of regional and perhaps national business leaders, and it can produce analyses that may expose reporting weaknesses.
5. Because regional leaders have an incentive program that targets revenue and profit by segment for their regions, any change to the way this is reported or to who controls the addition of costs affects their ability to achieve their objectives, which are tied to compensation.

We are not trying to resolve the issues here; we simply want to point out that the process we are undergoing to arrive at a long-term integrated improvement plan will inevitably arrive at conclusions and objectives that will be at odds with existing programs, incentives, and perhaps careers. Though we're not trying to be cavalier about this, these issues must be addressed and resolved, or the organization will continue to send out conflicting messages and will fail to design a long-term improvement program that will produce the desired results.

Again, when the conflict occurs at executive levels, the need becomes even more acute to identify and design solutions that both keep the program on track and manage the process of changing issues at the executive level, such that the program enjoys the full support of each functional leader. It has been our experience that when emotional reactions created by positional negotiating have been taken out of the discussion, it is possible to reduce the discussion to reasonably accurate estimates of financial results produced by competing designs. It is important to reduce as many of the outputs to financial terms as possible, including estimates of less tangible impacts on sales potential or research. The more this is reduced to financial terms, the more compelling the case for change to derive positive business results.

 SUMMARY

As the outputs from these discussions ensue, the evaluation team will create a list of all instances where issues or challenges that are found could ultimately result in failure to resolve potential conflicts, thereby reducing the chances of the programs moving forward on schedule and on budget. Inevitably, there will be issues raised that will challenge the status quo for leadership, and these can either be addressed in open discussions, if the culture of the organization will allow for it, or they can be worked through in individual conversations with the top executive overseeing this program (usually, the CEO, the COO, or the CFO of the organization). The governance program we will establish in the next chapter will have day-to-day responsibility to work through issues as they arise; however, fundamental stumbling blocks will be known from the start, and potentially fatal flaws in the organization dealt with before they result in failure for the program and possibly for the business.

It is unusual in our experience that these characteristics and behaviors in organizations of any size are not known. It is also unusual in our experience that the leadership organization doesn't collectively choose to believe that they are either resolved or being addressed in some way. It is typically easier when the issues are actually not known, because rigid political positions have not been taken in most cases. Yet this is not what we have experienced. In the next step in this process (Chapter 10), we are going to design, establish, and implement a function within the organization to work with issues as they arise and to help manage resolving them when they may not have been identified at the front end of the process or may have been identified and specifically assigned to this function to manage resolution.

The more issues with the potential to create conflicts that could derail or delay the program that can be identified and resolved at this point, the more likely that the governance process can proceed with a reasonable chance of success. There will always be issues of timelines, costs, designs, and others that will occur as more is learned about the organization, the software, and potential solutions to issues that are raised. We are establishing a new politic for the organization that makes these disputed issues discussable in Chris Argyris's terminology and creates a forum for resolution.

10

Developing a Governance Process

"In order to provide customers with "more for less," a firm must become more adept at managing the performance of the firm's large, cross-functional processes in a deliberate and collaborative way. This management practice has become known as 'process management.' It's not just about reengineering. It's not just about Six Sigma. Certainly tool sets such as reengineering and Six Sigma have some role to play, but process management is more about a business process orientation throughout the enterprise, and it calls for a dramatically different way of thinking and acting. In a nutshell, it requires that leaders have both the right attitude and aptitude to define, improve, and manage the company's value chain."

—*Andrew Spanyi*, More for Less: The Power of Process Management

INTRODUCTION

The structure and execution of a governance process is as essential to the success of a program as the project team members or the tools that are selected. In Part II of this book, we discussed five business aspects that require a project team to both view and analyze these business components from different perspectives than in the past (changes in cognitive level views of the organization). A process was then proposed for analyzing the information that was developed during evaluations of these five components to determine the interactions between each combination that may affect how a program can deal with issues as they arise.

On all projects, there are decisions that must be made while designing and implementing change that will need to be properly and respectfully managed, lest they derail the best of intentions. The existence and organization of a program governance function is key to the way in which projects are prepared and executed. More commonly, however, project organizations are "built to formula" around PMP principles (Project Management Professional certification from the Project Management Institute), rather than being built to manage decision making in a highly complex organization, which are found in all cross-functional organizations. This is not meant to disparage PMP skill sets, because they are crucial to project success; however, they are often the highest management level that projects operate at when a more extensive governance function is required, due to the pervasive effect these programs have on all aspects of organizations.

When talking about long-term program governance, we mean a separate function from what is included on a typical project team. The governance structure is consistent with and aligned with basic PMP concepts, but the difference is in how "alive" the management process is to drive decision making and organizational change management, particularly in support of executive levels.

LEADERSHIP CHALLENGES

This is the point where modern views of transformational leadership encounter knowledge and skill gaps within executive ranks. Although it is unreasonable to suggest that senior executives become expert in designing business processes, it is reasonable to suggest that leaders in an ERP-enabled world have to understand the conceptual challenges and need to establish a process to deal with these issues. This is necessary to ensure that the organization remains focused on improving business results.

Just as a dynamic leadership team will certainly not forget to include understanding of markets or strategic plans, the leadership team and vision must also include a component that deals with using modern knowledge of business process integration to turn IT applications costs into a continuous business improvement program. This is required both to improve current performance and to include and incorporate actions taken as a part of strategic plans, which may include acquisitions, divestitures, new capital investment, and much more. The governance process must be incorporated into an organizational leadership approach to deal with transformational issues in the transition to or management within an ERP platform.

PROGRAM GOVERNANCE PROCESS

The governance process that will be described here has been designed and used successfully to manage a large, complex, fixed-price project successfully, arguably the most challenging of environments. It features three distinct functions with clear relationships, authority, and responsibility to one another and to the overall program:

- Executive Steering Committee
- Program Governance Office
- Project Management Office

None of these are new. All are used in one form or another on every project. However, the elements described here, as a set, are designed to work through political processes that affect every program or project. As we discuss each, as well as how they are executed, real-world examples will be provided to demonstrate how this governance organization is used to deal with some very serious issues that frequently arise. It is not only for large complex projects but even on very small projects where several components may be invested in one person. Each of the functions is still important. To put it another way, it is not crucial that the elements we have here be named; it is not even important that the elements involve additional or even different people. What is important is that the program management organization must consider each of these, understand the roles that each plays in the success of the program, and clearly define how each element will operate, both individually and collectively.

Executive Steering Committee

The Executive Steering Committee (ESC), a standing committee, must be led by the most senior business leader who exercises overall responsibility for the areas affected. This statement should not be a revelation at all because it is included in virtually every text on leadership, change, or project management. Amazingly, though, it is still overlooked, underemphasized, or intentionally ignored in many circumstances. In fact, this is the normal starting point for any discussion of transformational change projects, particularly those that involve or are based on ERP applications. Typically, this person may be the chief operating officer (COO) or the equivalent for an enterprise-wide program (or if the scope is more limited, the senior officer responsible for the areas being affected). Because ERP applications generally start with the basic back-office integration engine, where financials, logistics, and HR intersect, a continuous improvement program will nearly always involve all of these functions and therefore be led from the COO or similar position, regardless of what the title may be. There are a number of reasons that this often doesn't happen, but it is absolutely key to the ultimate success of the program. If the COO and CFO positions are equivalent, at times this can be led jointly by the two. Yet the tacit agreement must be that they will work together to present a single leadership approach to the rest of the ESC. It should also be noted that often the stated reason for delegating this to a more junior position is due to time constraints. If this committee is used properly, however, the time spent on this leadership function will be time well spent.

The ESC must include all executive stakeholders, meaning that for each function affected by the changes or the integration, the most senior leader in that group must be assigned to the ESC. Many times, and for many reasons, leaders will delegate this assignment down in their organization, which is nearly always problematic for the intended role this group needs to play. If used properly, the ESC can be instrumental in enhancing the visibility and control by senior leaders without threatening the political environment. Furthermore, if the program office discussed in the next section operates properly, the time burden for participation on this committee, just as with the chairperson, should be manageable. Problems may, however, occur when the dynamic of decision making, which is discussed later in this chapter, is not executed properly.

In any event, the top leader in each function must be engaged as a committee member and, equally important, must actually attend the meetings. This will happen when the ESC chair makes his or her own commitment to personally attend and sets expectations for the rest of the committee members. Often, the aversion of this by senior leaders is due to the tendency for this group to be used by subordinates to engage in highly political decision making. As we will demonstrate in further discussion, however, this is not how the committee should function.

A personal example of how this committee should operate will be useful. Decades ago, I had the privilege of working as staff for a very senior general officer while serving in the U.S. Air Force. My reason for coming to this assigned base was to work through some political issues with other generals on topics affecting the conduct of the Vietnam War. As part of my duties, my job was to work with staff officers for the other generals to arrive at mutually agreed-on positions on the issues. The objective was that when the generals gathered, they would present a cohesive face to other participants as if there had been agreement from the start. Clearly, there was an order of rank; however, the participants crossed major organizational boundaries and were not simple superior-subordinate relationships. The discussion and negotiation process went back and forth and took several days before resulting in agreement. Yet the process of gaining consensus between the generals illustrated several principles:

1. The agreed-on positions would not have been possible if it were not for the impending meeting with the larger group (time constraints help, as in all negotiations). This was the event that created the necessity for all of the staff work to be done, the negotiated final position to be agreed to, and the final deal to be cut. This is a key point that deals with other leadership teams overcoming intransigent political obstacles to gain consensus positions and remain on the critical path.

2. Placing senior officers (military or civilian) in the position of public and political disputes in open forum was to be avoided at all costs. Failure to do so could prove embarrassing to both the officers who won the battle and those who lost and could have long-term implications for future decisions. Ultimately, one of the officers was senior to the others and could have imposed a solution on the group; however, that method would have clearly led to less than the desired results.

3. At the meeting itself, the agreed-on mutual position was laid out and questions invited, but the unanimity of the senior group allowed the meeting to appear to present a military command decision. This is important in the military; however, it is also important in industry. To ask for a debate between senior leaders in public may very well lead to winners

and losers and potential embarrassment to many. The ESC is subject to the same rules.

4. Decisions that are controversial need to be discussed and resolutions agreed to in smaller forums before the ESC meets so that the decision can be presented to the whole group, mostly to communicate what is happening. If this discussion starts to become confrontational, it must be stopped, taken offline, and resolved. If the discussion is on the critical path, this may require haste, but still the ESC cannot become a meeting that senior leaders avoid because of risk of embarrassment.

Unfortunately, it is not unusual for executive leadership to treat this process like an IT project and delegate all of the control to the CIO/VP-IT, which may satisfy the need for executive control but avoids the real mechanism for achieving ROI—organizational change management across the enterprise. Delegated to IT (unless the CIO is seen as one of the top business leaders who just happens to be responsible for IT), this often results in degrading the ability to drive decision making on business process design, as well as management of the process during the project, which will encounter roadblocks at every turn.

How IT is used to define business processes and produce business benefits must become a component of the education and knowledge of all senior leaders and also become a part of the never-ending personal development process, as discussed in Chapter 8. A well-staffed ESC that meets regularly to provide information and understanding among executives can be an important part of that process. Even in companies that start out with a properly designed and functioning ESC often slide over time into a trap where more junior managers attend as substitutes, where conflict becomes the nature of the meeting, and where leadership becomes less and less effective at keeping the program on track. As described in Chapter 2, the role of leadership in an integrated business world must evolve to understanding the issues around cross-functional business decisions and keeping these decisions on the critical path. Without this understanding, projects are often dead from the start.

Program Governance Office

The function of the Program Governance Office, which may be a person or a group, is the least understood and is very often not included in either the project or the longer-term program design. It is, however, the Program Governance Office's role to have ultimate responsibility for keeping the programs on track. As timelines start to slide or miss targets, the Program Governance Office must be able to identify the trend early, when steps can still be taken to maintain the project schedule. There is an inviolate principle (critical path management) included in all project management education, which is embedded but frequently underappreciated. This principle provides insight into the role of this governance component:

1. A critical path should always be defined early in project planning. This path reflects key decisions or checkpoints in the project plan that must be completed by a certain date to avoid delays due to dependencies later in the project timeline. Creation of the critical path document is often done superficially or perfunctorily, such that the document contains items that are really not part of the critical path or may leave out items that do affect the project timeline. The creation and testing of this timeline is one of the first items that the Program Governance Office deals with. Otherwise, one ends up with what has been called the Christopher Columbus School of Management, described earlier in this book.

   Far too infrequently, critical path documents are created and used as effective tools to manage a program. This is not typically because of lack of effort but results from too little knowledge of the relationship between decisions and work scheduling. It is also important that at the very beginning of the project, the critical path document is reviewed with and agreed to by each of the senior executives involved. There is nothing more destructive to a project timeline than to get to a critical path decision and have the leadership team engage in a discussion about how it really isn't a critical decision. It is necessary to get this established up front so that the focus can remain on the key issue at hand.

2. The Program Governance Office is responsible for monitoring the progress of the project team on a continuous basis, knowing when critical path decisions are approaching and knowing before dates are missed of the likelihood of that happening.

   Being closely tied to all of the senior leadership allows the program manager to facilitate discussions before the critical date and gain consensus, whatever is necessary. It is worth pointing out that consensus doesn't always mean everyone is happy with the choice. However, the decision is being made within a political culture, and consensus, in this case, may simply imply that each participant understands the decision, what it means to his or her organization, and will support it. In order for this to be accomplished, other cultural and political issues discovered and considered during the analytical phase must be addressed by executives with the help of the program manager.

3. When a critical path decision is approaching and it appears that the date may be missed, the program officer notifies the responsible leaders; it is not unusual for participants to indicate that they need more time to get the decision made correctly.

   This is where trust in the critical path document, as well as in the Program Governance Office, is crucial, because any delay will cause the project to be delayed, by definition of the term *critical path*. This would require a revision of the completion date, additional costs incurred at whatever the weekly run rate (average weekly expenditures) is, and potential revision to the Return on Investment calculations. It is simply a case of understanding what the impact will be at the time that action to prevent this impact can still be taken.

4. When failure to make a decision regarding the delay of a project becomes critical, the Program Governance Office ensures that this decision is elevated to the level of the organization that has the authority to commit the additional costs for the business.

   Due to the potentially large weekly cost being committed, this potential critical path failure inevitably rises to the very top levels, particularly because it is likely that additional costs for this program can also have an impact on other investment opportunities. Usually, leaders who fail to make decisions on the critical path do not have the signatory authority to commit these additional funds by themselves; however, their inability to make the decision does exactly that, as surely as building a new manufacturing line does.

5. As stated earlier and worth reiterating here, the key to making this work is creating a believable critical path document early in the program, gaining understanding and agreement on its use at the start, and foreseeing difficult decisions early enough that they can be made on time.

   The intent is not to always make everyone happy, but as much as possible to reduce conflict to something that is quantifiable. Most senior executives can accept decisions that they may not like or advocate, if they believe that the ultimate financial results will be better for the company. This is the job of the program management function.

The Program Governance Office is generally a group that is typically co-led by a senior executive who is responsible to the ESC for the successful execution of the program, along with the senior consulting leader(s) responsible for delivery. This may be the CIO (chief information officer) of the affected organization (by role, if not title) and may include one of their staff members who has specific expertise in the software being implemented. Assuming that there is a systems integrator (consultancy) involved, the senior leader(s) from the consulting company will also be part of this function. While the client program leader is directly responsible to the ESC for program execution, there is also a shared responsibility with the lead person from the systems integrator. It is important that all members of this function have the confidence and support from the executive team and that there is open, private communication between each of them, because many of the issues may be difficult and may require trust to arrive at a satisfactory conclusion. It has been our experience that this relationship can be difficult because the consulting leader often doesn't understand this role and because the business leaders don't establish trust with the consultant.

The role of the Program Governance Office is to maintain day-to-day oversight of the project and become involved in defining, discussing, and negotiating decisions on key process design issues. Typically, this group (or person) meets with project team leaders formally once a week, when all of the project metrics are produced and explained by the project managers. This provides an opportunity and a platform to focus on metrics, such as progress against the critical path, review of both issues, and the decision logs, and to either push to ensure that these are in sync with one another or elect to become engaged in resolving roadblocks. Other activities of the Program Governance Office include

- Discussion of proposed change orders to determine whether the change is prudent and therefore should be approved by the ESC or whether another approach may allow the program to stay in scope and/or on time. The ultimate responsibility to maintain the scope of the program, both to include prevention of scope creep and to avoid shortfalls, is with this group.
- Review of all program metrics that are agreed on at the start. Typically, this includes cost of consultants, cost of internal resources, expenses, and so on.
- Providing daily access by all members of the Program Governance Office to deal with unexpected issues as they occur or to deal with the inability to finalize decisions that affect the critical path and additional costs being incurred. When the program is running well, this can be a weekly process or when difficult issues of design or execution arise, direct daily access can

be demanding and busy. The issue is that the attention to the process must be available at all times where involvement is required by the main participants and decision makers.

In many projects, where design and resistance issues are encountered and not successfully resolved, providing daily access is one of two governance functions that is quite often overlooked, the other being the commitment and involvement of senior leadership. Keeping the focus on large complex programs is never easy and requires commitment and attention on key critical path challenges, and this function is designed to see that it happens. A few organizations have performed this governance function quite informally and in an open environment; however, these organizations are typically not very large or complex.

In larger, more complex organizations, organizational relationships, culture, and politics become more difficult to manage. More often, this governance function is fully engaged in negotiations with functional executives and with helping to resolve issues that must be addressed at higher levels. At times, personal issues, such as incentive compensation or scope of responsibility, can be negatively affected for individual leaders. Any of these governance functions that are ignored can create problems that prevent programs from staying on track.

Project Management Office

This is the day-to-day operational hub of the project. It includes the project manager(s) responsible for the overall project and the project manager responsible for the internal recording, tracking, and reporting of program metrics and may include other key stakeholders. Typically, a project will be divided into several functional teams and, depending on size, may have several leaders who must work together or may be small enough that many responsibilities are combined and assigned to one person. Either way, there are team leaders, which may be as simple as a consultant and an empowered business representative, or may be many times that size. There is a lot of literature about how to design implementation teams and projects, all consistent with materials produced by the Project Management Institute, ERP vendors, and many others. Remember what was stated earlier in this book: The use of qualified resources and proper project management tools is assumed for our purposes.

Most literature that discusses "What makes projects fail?" includes issues with the organization and the execution of this function. Yet many projects still fail, and many more fail to achieve the business benefits that the projects are capable of producing. This is not typically because the project managers don't know basic project management principles or techniques. It is much more often because the overall program has not developed and established roles to deal with all levels of management to ensure that decisions get made in a timely manner and are based on an understanding of the business results expected from those decisions. The person who is an expert at managing day-to-day details of project planning is not often the same person who is able to establish credibility with senior leaders to help them deal with serious political and cultural issues. Some of the very best project managers simply either aren't comfortable dealing with these issues or are stymied by the potential job- and career-threatening aspects of possibly disappointing senior leaders.

Although this function is not for the faint of heart, we often place outstanding technicians (PMP certified and well equipped with analytical methods of tracking and reporting on progress) in direct contact with senior leaders who operate on an entirely different level of management, and then we expect positive results. Following this path may lead to success, but it is certainly the exception and not the rule.

The Project Governance Office must include a functional project manager, who may be from the consulting contractor or may have some consulting background, and a technical/business project manager who will be responsible for all of the support functions, such as RICEF (reports, interfaces, conversions, enhancements, and forms), organizational change management, training, and the gathering and reporting on all project metrics. Along with these, there will be a client project manager who takes daily direction from the CIO (or similar executive) and has direct access when necessary to the ESC chairperson.

In the case of large projects, there should be a project office manager who has daily responsibility for expenditures, project logistics, and all reporting against work plans and the critical path. This person is not ultimately in charge of the overall project but supports the project managers and provides the eyes and ears of the Program Governance Office to stay on top of issues and project flows as they occur. Obviously, on smaller projects this may be incorporated into a single person. The issue really becomes, however, if your key project leaders spend all day buried in spreadsheets and metrics, who is left to work on resolving cross-functional design issues between departments, which is the most challenging issue? Both are crucial to the success of the project and may be conflicting when invested in one person. Obviously, this depends on project size. As indicated at the beginning of our discussion, there is a lot of literature on the "hows" and "whys" of setting up good project management functions and selecting project managers. It is not our intent to repeat that here. What is left out of the literature, however, are instructions on working through leadership issues that often may cause ERP programs to fail, which is different than the experience included in PMP skill sets.

 ## CONTINUOUS IMPROVEMENT PROGRAMS

The dynamics described herein of continuous improvement programs are valid for all projects, regardless of size, and the actual design and assignments of these continuous improvement programs will depend on all of the aspects of corporate leadership described in Part II. Because this is an element that must be performed by one means or another, continuous improvement programs are important to think of as a distribution of assigned responsibilities, rather than as an additional cost for another layer of management. If continuous improvement programs do result in additional costs, these costs should be viewed as adding components of governance that were simply lacking in the current project plans. How can this be applied to longer or even permanent programs?

Referring back to Chapter 3, the explosion of ERP applications during the last few decades has created an opportunity to flatten the investment curve with a focus on Return on Investment. Although this requires a change in the perception of how organizations plan for and execute changes associated with business processes, the opportunity to flatten the investment curve and create a long-term or permanent view of using IT strategy to derive continuous business benefits has arrived. One must consider the implications for this program governance model in continuous improvement programs. Specifically, one now has to consider the following needs.

- Five business aspects (evergreen)
- Upgrades
- Additions to the ERP platform
- Collection of work request
- Introduction of new technologies

Five Business Aspects

The five analyses created in Part II of this book are also not static but continue to change and evolve over time. Some of this evolution will be the result of organizational development work in areas that are identified as possible improvements. Some will be due to a natural evolution created by turnover in leadership ranks so that different objectives and needs will either be added or deleted, and some will come about as organizational needs are met or become apparent from earlier successes. The program office has the responsibility to see that these analyses remain evergreen and to lead discussions when changes to the organization create the need for further evaluation. It is important that new executives also be brought into the process and be enlisted as supporters. If issues with new executives arise, this function can help navigate changes in executive relationships before they become fatal to the overall program.

Upgrades

Upgrades can now be broken up into smaller pieces that allow for upgrading one or two components of the suite at a time, and upgrade strategy is critical. This strategy must include a review of the contents of upgrades, which may involve new or changed functionality and comparison to organizational needs in the Return on Investment analysis. Prioritization, scheduling, and staffing of these sequential or perhaps overlapping projects will be permanent, unless one theorizes that the organization will reach a point where further improvements are no longer possible, which would most likely require the business world to become more static, which is not a likely event.

Due to the explosion of capability in ERP applications, if one gets to this point, perhaps one should think harder. At the very least, markets (sales, materials, human resources) and clients are changing, which will require constantly rethinking the business processes to ensure that one remains as close as possible to his or her clients' needs. This was much of the reason for earlier programs, such as centralization or decentralization. Designed and managed effectively, the continued implementation and use of ERP applications can replace the artificial programs that were used to drive change in the past. This doesn't mean that centralization or the reverse may not still be important, only that it will be part of the overall program that will determine change management directions based on continuous improvements.

Additions to the ERP Platform

A company may not have implemented CRM or SCM and/or perhaps has divested or acquired a business. The work to incorporate these large changes into the corporate culture and applications must be managed as part of the work stream, because the objective is for the total enterprise to be integrated and coordinated based on an expected Return on Investment. There is no reason that these corporate-event driven projects should not be held to the same standards, even though it may be more difficult to establish the return on divestitures, other than those included in the business case for doing it in the first place. Any financial plan for events such as divestitures should include the IT costs of demerging systems into the evaluation, and these changes should still be managed as part of the larger project stream.

Collection of Work Requests

Every ERP system we have encountered has collected a large, unmanageable number of individual work requests. These requests may be as simple as adding a field on a report to production of a new analysis or adding storage locations for new warehouse facilities somewhere in the system. The administrative process for managing these is typically that the majority of the requests get prioritized into a queue and either never have any chance of being worked on or never get collated with other similar requests where collectively they could become a project based on business improvements.

One of the most serious issues with the acceptance of ERP platforms is that this queue is a constant source of irritation and politics and, in many cases, the requests really don't make any sense in the first place. These issues could often more properly be closed by retraining, further education, or simply saying that it is inconsistent with the new view of how the business will be managed. The queue itself becomes an issue for discontent and is seen as an indication that the system doesn't work, further eroding support throughout the workforce.

Introduction of New Technologies

There is a constant stream of new technology solutions, often for problems or issues that don't exist or, even if they do, the need for them has not been identified and quantified. It is important that this permanent function also be responsible for continuously evaluating new technology or capability that is being developed, relate those advancements to creating business value (Return on Investment), and include them in strategic and periodic reevaluations of the project stream.

Thus, the inclusion of a continuous improvement program as a permanent part of managing the IT applications that support and, in some ways, define the business is necessitated by the current world, where innovation, new business needs, changing markets, and necessity to maintain systems are coming at us faster and faster. This management of the IT applications will only become more frenetic as time passes. There is already so much value the current technology can contribute and yet has not. As a permanent function within the business, continuous improvement programs will, over time, incorporate knowledge of and competency in managing this powerful IT asset, such that it becomes part of basic leadership toolsets.

 ## SUMMARY

It is possible, depending on the size and complexity of the program or project, for some of these functions to be performed by one person. On larger programs or projects, there may be large staffs supporting each function. The size, however, is important only to the extent that the governance process be scaled to reflect the size of the project or the program. Appropriateness of the scale is determined by how effectively the process can be used by leadership to manage the political environment and the work organization to accomplish the goals. If one looks back at any successful project from the past, one will see that each of these functions has been addressed, some formally and some perhaps by one very visible leader, but addressed nevertheless.

On a small project some years ago, all 11 members of the corporate office staff were part time on the project team. All of the responsibilities of the program and project offices fell on the consulting program leader and the client project manager. Unlike conventional wisdom as it pertains to smaller organizations being easier to work with, however, the key success factor on this program was organizational change management, because each of the key staff members had designed his or her current business processes and was emotionally committed to them. Actual configuration and demo and testing of solutions were simplified because it was done in two- and three-person teams. Finally, data conversions were done manually, and various master data elements were only created as they were needed after the go-live date. Not a desirable situation, but in this case, it worked well. The point here is that on very small projects, the same issues and problems arise and the same organizational and personal dynamics must be managed. This, however, need not necessarily add costs of complexity to a project.

On a larger implementation ($35M fixed price, full suite in 19 months), the full governance process described earlier was in place and proved capable of keeping the program on track to successful completion. In this case, the overall project team numbered close to 100, but the process was the same, just larger and involving more people. Designing and implementing the program governance described here allows an organization of any size to identify issues and challenges that need to be addressed and allows the ERP applications to deliver the planned Return on Investment. Conversely, if the leadership structure of the organization isn't going to perform in support of the programs and achieve intended objectives, this can be identified early in the program and either dealt with or cause expectations to be redefined. It is always better to recognize early in the program that the organization is not ready to make the necessary commitments for success and to realign expectations accordingly.

CHAPTER ELEVEN

Organizational Change Management

"Today, systems thinking is needed more than ever because we are becoming overwhelmed by complexity. Perhaps for the first time in history, humankind has the capacity to create far more information than anyone can absorb, to foster far greater interdependency than anyone can manage, and to accelerate change far faster than anyone's ability to keep pace. Certainly the scale of complexity is without precedent. All around us are examples of 'systemic breakdowns.'"

—*Peter Senge,* The Fifth Discipline

 INTRODUCTION

The primary discussion in this chapter will focus directly on how to use organizational change management (OCM) programs at all levels of the organization, including the executive suite, to keep programs on track and to achieve the intended Return on Investment. Material presented in earlier chapters discussed the integration of the output of various elements, resulting in a governance process sufficient to manage these important elements, which include Return on Investment, business process analysis, business culture analysis, IT strategy development, and workforce readiness.

These elements must now be analyzed as we design a continuous improvement approach to ERP implementation and management. With the understanding of organizational processes developed and with an effective governance program established, our attention can now turn to the issue of (OCM), essentially the framework within which all organizational change occurs, whether accidentally or purposefully.

 ## EXPANDING THE ROLE OF OCM

For decades, well-established and well-led projects have included some form of OCM practices within project teams. Yet nearly all of the attention has been focused on how to gain acceptance of the new and changed processes within the worker community. Little, if any, attention has been paid to getting decision support mechanisms built in support of redesign and implementation within the executive ranks. There are several significant reasons for this:

- Project staff is uncomfortable dealing with executives on highly political issues.
- Analysis of organizational processes is rarely done.
- The project is seen as an IT project, not owned by the business team.
- There is no trusted adviser to work with conflict at the ESC level.
- Decision makers are not on the ESC—it is staffed at too low a level.

Exhibit 11.1 illustrates the process that should be used in designing the governance and change management functions in order to successfully achieve Return on Investment targets. Exhibit 11.1 also shows how governance and change management surround the new plan and provide the tools and staff to ensure success.

A comprehensive continuous improvement plan must be developed that flattens the investment curve, bases each sequential or overlapping project on Return on Investment, and has established a governance process. This comprehensive continuous improvement plan must oversee the program and deal with how issues in organizational change affect all levels of the organization.

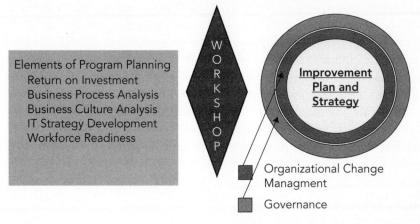

Elements of Program Planning
Return on Investment
Business Process Analysis
Business Culture Analysis
IT Strategy Development
Workforce Readiness

WORKSHOP

Improvement
Plan and
Strategy

Organizational Change
Managment

Governance

EXHIBIT 11.1   Improvement Plan and Strategy with Elements of Program Planning
Source: © 2012 Arthur Worster, Worster Associates, LLC. Reproduced with permission.

It is time now to turn to the dynamics of executing the program. If the steps to execute the program have been done effectively, the following will be true:

- All improvement programs have either been incorporated into the continuous improvement program stream, or they have been identified and tagged as able to operate independently without conflicting with the larger program.
- Executives responsible for each of the functional areas included in the scope (more than likely representing every area of the enterprise) have been involved in the process of establishing the program, and all of the executives are fully invested in the Executive Steering Committee.
- Clear objectives and methodologies have been established for designing new business processes.
- The need to deal with change within the cultural/political process is accepted and supported.
- Educational programs have been established to close the knowledge gaps at all levels of the organization.
- A governance function has been established with the explicit responsibility to work with senior executives to resolve issues that arise between functions or with issues such as compensation, objectives, and career planning.

It is now time to move the process forward. Defined earlier in this book was the role leadership must play in ensuring that the knowledge of the internal business processes and IT applications that support them exists within the broader enterprise. Also, one must remember that the role of the leader who is establishing long-term strategic goals of the business is not to necessarily understand this in detail, but to ensure that the governance program established includes the necessary skills and acceptance to manage this process successfully. This is the key.

The role of leaders is to provide the vision and not become entrapped in day-to-day details of the operation. A leader's role is also to ensure that the other leaders in the organization are aligned around the goals. John Kotter points out the difference between leadership and management, and this is a good case of the changing focus on leadership in an integrated business world, where a large portion of the organizational staff has not had the opportunity or experience to work cross-functionally.

 ## ORGANIZATIONAL CHANGE MANAGEMENT WITH LEADERS

How does the change management process work at higher levels? A typical program scope document will often contain a statement on how OCM should work that reads something like this: We will establish an OCM function as part of the program team to deal with the effects of changes on the workforce. This will include skills assessments and focus groups, along with communication and training for the levels to be affected.

What this doesn't deal with is what happens when the project team members have worked through the business process designs and developed a design that has a negative effect on one or more senior leaders. This happens frequently when moving to a fully integrated business process. It is typical that the political organization at the staff level will act to prevent resolution of the issue, not intentionally, but because of problem resolution conflicts that remain unresolved.

There is an important book on this subject by Chris Argyris titled *Overcoming Organizational Defenses*, which is extremely insightful. Instead of outright refusing to accept the outcome, the executive often asks the project team designee to go back to the group and find something that "works better" or, worse yet, sends messages that position the team members to fight for politically expedient solutions. The real need is for executives who find themselves in this position to accept the proposed solution, understand the personal results of these designs, and have an open invitation to discuss with their superiors the unintended negative consequences, such as objectives, compensation, promotion, and so on. This solution, however, is often a difficult, if not impossible, political discussion and one where the executive neither really understands the positive effects of the recommended changes nor, more important, understands the negative effects of other solutions on the enterprise.

THE TRUSTED ADVISER

The Program Governance Office, part of the governance program that must be established, provides a clearinghouse for issues as they arise and provides an individual or individuals with both the credibility and the responsibility to facilitate in these discussions. In previous discussions, the responsibility for staff functions was to work through issues that have an effect on executives privately, in small groups, or with top leadership. The intent is that these discussions are never allowed to result in public conflict, which is both embarrassing to the executives and inevitably leads to dysfunction in executive-staff relationships. Unfortunately, it is almost a certainty that at one or more points during the project, when a proposed solution by the project team is not readily accepted by the functional leadership, the conversation turns to "bad" culture, politics, or organization.

The fact is that there is a "correct" resolution to design issues for any organization, and it is the combination of logical design, organizational direction (leadership vision), and practical relationships between leaders that determines what the correct resolution should be. The governance and change management processes cannot be viewed as disrespectful of any of these interests. This is why the Program Governance Office must be led by a person, or persons, who have the trust of ESC members and who must be able to work through the issues diplomatically, in order to arrive at the solution that is the best for the overall business and to help resolve unintended consequences in a manner that allows for optimal solutions for the organization as a whole. There are times when the vision of the organization may overrule short-term benefits for the longer-term good, and project teams don't often have that perspective or latitude.

CHANGE MANAGEMENT PROCESS

Many participants have differing views of what OCM is. These differing views may include how one plans and prepares to manage organizational change, what person or function should be responsible, and whether OCM is going to be hard (or even possible) to manage successfully within the organization. The premise remains, however, that if one is seeking improved business results, one must change business processes. This does not mean, however, that there won't be times when design decisions seem shortsighted. Thus, it is necessary that the resolution process must have the respect of the larger organization.

Along this path, there are a series of decision points that are on the "critical path" and require choices. These are at both the project and the executive level. An examination must occur of the broader OCM process, and an evaluation must be made of how the tools and management of change are used, which affect every level of the business. The following four areas must be examined and evaluated:

1. Identify areas of intended change, up and down the organization.
2. Understand the components of the organization that will have to change.
3. Choose the tools that will have to be created and deployed to manage these changes.
4. Define the educational needs that will provide skill sets to optimize results.

Identify Areas of Intended Change, Up and Down the Organization

The crux of the issue is identifying the areas of intended change in the organization. Any time one is engaged in designing, implementing, or managing in an ERP environment, there will be design choices. These choices result in changed business processes. The changes go both ways—down to workers, and up to executives. Although significant effort has gone into developing tools to manage change processes in the workforce, the causes of failures more often occur at, or result from decisions or attitudes at, executive levels. These failures are not because senior executives don't care but because the resulting changes to the leadership process are not addressed or effectively managed. Also, the career paths and areas of expertise of senior executives have not necessarily included sufficient exposure to the systems and processes they will now have to employ, as discussed throughout this book.

Time spent working with these executives to redefine how they will manage their departments as part of the larger integrated business can prevent many of these issues and can turn resistance into support. It will also determine when a level of resistance may require convening several executives to work out an acceptable solution (better to know that up front, when there is still time to remain on the critical path). This process is addressed by the Program Governance Office. Here is an example of what happens too often as a result of decisions made by executive teams that do not fully understand the effects on the project teams.

While teaching an introductory ERP course some years ago, coauthor Art Worster asked the students how they were managing "reengineering" business processes, and here is roughly the discussion that ensued:

Class Group (actually, a group from one company): We aren't! Our management has decided that we are just going to implement the ERP application, but we aren't going to reengineer our processes.

Worster: Then, why do you think your organization is going to spend all of this money to get the new software implemented?

Class Group: Well, there are a lot of things that don't work very well, and ERP is going to fix them.

Worster: How do you think that is going to happen? What do you think is going to change so that these things get resolved?

Class Group: Well, the ERP program will provide us with business processes that straighten all of these things out.

Worster: You will find out that in any ERP program, organizational design, master data records design, design of transactions, and in many more areas, decisions will be made by the implementation team. How will these be made, if not by you?

Class Group: That's what the consultants are there for.

Worster: Are you really willing to turn all of these decisions over to consultants who have no knowledge of your business and will not be saddled with the results?

Class Group: No, of course we will not just turn it over to them. We will have to make those decisions as a team as the functionality is designed.

Worster: Please tell me again that you are not going to "reengineer" the business.

Class Group: Our executives discussed this, and this is the direction that they provided.

Unfortunately, this is a true story (nearly verbatim). Much has been learned about these systems over the years; however, various versions of this and a multitude of other similar questions still occur today. One should note that this set of instructions came from the senior leaders of the organization who were implementing the software. It is safe to say that none of the team members in the course (which included the project manager) had sufficient understanding or influence to tell the executives that further discussion was necessary. When a CIO of a leading company was asked his opinion of the ERP project he was engaged in leading some years ago, the CIO responded that he believed the most obvious characteristic was that it was "career limiting." The fact of the matter is that any ERP implementation will result in new business processes, if only because of logical relationships. Change management cannot occur at the team or worker levels of the organization; it has to start with the executive sponsorship and that requires a trusted adviser.

Program leaders, with experience and knowledge, can generally find high-quality consultants who are needed to execute configuration, can find teams of people who know the business well enough to make informed decisions on options, and can design, implement, and test the solutions. What continues to not be done well is gathering all of the change implications of these actions and execute plans to get the changed organization reengineered and implemented. We have learned to deal with this better at the user levels of organizations but not at the executive levels. All ERP applications require changes to business processes that must be understood by the leaders who will be affected. In most instances, the changes to business processes can be quantified in real economic terms where the business improvements of various options are implemented.

Understand the Components of the Organization That Will Have to Change

It is standard to include an OCM function within the project team. This is the person or the group whose responsibility is to work with the design teams, collect changes that will occur in the way business processes operate, translate changes in job roles and assignments, assess the skills that will be needed by workers, and develop training and communication programs to be used to deliver information about the new processes to affected workers. Better-constructed programs also include various focus groups to present proposed changes and get input and concerns back from group members that can then either be fed back to design teams or be used to develop the materials that are used to promote acceptance of the program as implementation nears. Well-experienced practitioners use many tools, and these are just a few. This is all good and necessary, and thankfully, the need is generally accepted for the use of these tools to promote and manage organizational change at the worker level.

Ultimately, this is a program of "expectations management" in describing the end goal of the program. Creating the sense of a need for change management requires defining and selling "expectations" that the affected community is willing to embrace. To be effective, this process starts when the program is announced and continues well past the implementation date. This strategy, however, has nearly always ignored one of the most important groups of stakeholders. It is much easier to sell a program down into the organization than it is to sell it up the management chain into top executive ranks, which requires a different set of skills, tools, and focus to manage properly.

Certain changes, necessitated by new software logic, result in the necessity to alter the way executives of the company must operate. These are numerous and result in decisions that require changes at the executive level on such diverse issues as what reports they will be able to see and how metrics may be rolled up, or they may even have a significant impact on how the enterprise is organized. In a typical project, resolution of these issues is left to departmental representatives on the project team, even though these team members may not have easy access to their top leaders, or, most important, they may not feel comfortable discussing issues such as these with the leaders. The crux of the matter, however, occurs when options at the top result in the necessity to change the way in which the organization is led and operates.

For example, this may result in the need to change executive objectives of which compensation programs may be built around. This is not typically a subject that lower-ranking subordinates can initiate or participate in, so another governance approach is necessary. It is likely that more projects fail because of these upward-looking OCM issues not being resolved than because of the inability to get the lower levels of the organization to accept new work processes. From our experience, most business leaders see their organization as a given, and changes in structures are generally prompted by other demands. It is necessary to gain acceptance within this group (the ESC, essentially), where there may be the need to change organizational structures based on the new cross-functional business processes that will evolve. This was not always the case, but today it is more prevalent.

Another example of senior leadership not fully comprehending the magnitude of change occurred some years ago. This example demonstrates why a deeper understanding of changes is so important. A manufacturing plant was having difficulty in getting its new ERP system to work "properly." After we met with the plant staff, it became apparent that the plant manager believed that one of the good things about the implementation was that there was no impact on employees, as far as people being laid off—not a bad start. On further investigation, it was discovered that in fact there were significant impacts that had not been recognized. In one example, the work of recording receiving transactions for chemical railcars, which had previously been accomplished by warehouse workers writing on scraps of paper that were sent to the front office for entry into the previous system, were now being recorded real-time on computers at the receiving dock, which was certainly a different work environment from the front office. It turned out that this had increased the workload of receiving department workers to the point where an additional worker was required and had decreased the work in the front office to the point where there was an excess worker.

One can only guess that someone had determined that this meant there were no net impacts. However, the receiving workers were strong guys who had to use hand winches to move railcars up and down the siding and who had no computer skills whatsoever. The office workers were women and some of the most senior employees of the plant, who had worked in an office environment for 30 years or more. This was certainly not about gender but about strength and work environment. To believe that there were no personnel impacts on the workforce would require the plant leaders to have been oblivious to the OCM needs of the project. Suffice it to say, there were significant changes required that had to be managed, starting with the plant leadership.

Choose the Tools That Will Have to Be Created/Deployed to Manage These Changes

What are the tools that are needed to address these issues? As discussed, tools and programs are available to address the issues of collecting current work processes, new work processes, an analysis of the change required, communication/training programs to prepare and support the workforce, and others. As stated, what is not addressed effectively is OCM at the executive level(s). When a team is engaged in the configuration phase of an ERP project, and when the scope has been clearly defined, the unanticipated choices or options for higher-level organizational issues become clearer, along with the rationale for the necessity of changes. When left to lower-level team leaders, this results in discussion within functional silos. Left to project managers, this occurs at ESC meetings and may result in arguments or deferred decisions, primarily because the issues that are raised go too deep into the political structure of the organization to be resolved in open session.

So, the Program Governance Office becomes the small empowered function tasked with managing OCM upward to get resolution of critical path decisions. There are many good examples of this to study, including the following.

Inventory Control

During the development of a common inventory control system that incorporates both positive purchase price variance objectives of the procurement function and raw material inventory management objectives of the manufacturing function, the challenge is to find a process that creates an optimal solution. Because the two executives (typically, they operate as two separate departments) may be compensated on performance against competing targets, resolution will require changing organizational responsibilities and objectives. It will require changing the target metric to total cost of inventory, which includes purchase price variance and costs associated with working capital for inventory. This methodology often results in a decision whether to have the new function report to one or another of the executives, with obvious personal and organizational implications.

Management Accounting

Another example is when an organization has grown through acquisition and is now being consolidated under one system. One of the merging business units is organized functionally, where departmental cost budgets are the primary management tools used for evaluation and reporting. In addition, the sales department might be judged on revenue created. In this system, the only place that profit is reported and managed is at the division staff level, which is a shared responsibility among the staff officers. The second business unit is organized in market segments, where leaders are evaluated based on gross profit (revenue less costs), and the primary management tool is either profit center reporting or segment profitability.

The project team, in consultation with the CFO, will usually determine which of the financial approaches is preferred, and the new approach will be agreed on. Regardless of what the decision is, the results will require significant change in the approach and the management structure of some executives. Although this may seem obvious, the process of talking with senior executives to figure out how to change their management approach and to identify reports and analytics they will need to see is often ignored. If the senior executives responsible for a functional or a business area are not comfortable with this process, they find it difficult to send positive messages to their organizations.

In mergers and consolidations, there is nearly always significant disruption at executive levels, where there may be redundancy in positions. To expect this process to be in any way benign, when careers are threatened and there will necessarily be winners and losers, is unrealistic. What is realistic, however, is that the executive teams accept that the ERP program must be executed within the cultural/political/organizational structure of the business and that the relationship between competition and the optimization of business processes must operate simultaneously. This, left unaddressed, can lead to anything from mild pain and confusion to total resistance. The Program Governance Office in the three-tiered governance process is the group specifically designated to deal with these issues as they arise and are defined by the project as it evolves. Upward focus on OCM is a key component of successful implementation. It does not happen by accident.

Define the Educational Needs That Will Provide Skill Sets to Optimize Results

It is necessary to evaluate the knowledge that is required of a project team to get these issues resolved. Certainly, cross-functional process knowledge throughout the team is essential to ensure that design options that are constructed represent a process that will optimally support the entire organization. There must be some cross-functional training conducted to provide knowledge of the consequences of actions in one function on another. Some ERP vendors have programs that address this, and in other cases, it may be necessary to create one.

Next, one needs to ensure that he or she has a support team (consultants, for the most part) whose members are absolute experts in the options of how to configure the system to achieve business results. In simple designs, this probably doesn't matter, but when one is involved in complex designs that affect how the overall enterprise will operate and will potentially require rewriting executive compensation programs, one had better have all of the knowledge available to ensure that he or she can meet the needs, and ensuring the qualifications of the consultants is a key part of that knowledge.

Finally, all of this is about operating the business, not about simple IT-supported transactional processes. Just as one can send leaders to educational opportunities from seminars to M.B.A. programs, one needs to ensure that these individual development programs include business education around how ERP functionality can be used to support business changes and how that can lead to a Return on Investment for companies. This can include seminars built around a particular company's functionality. Or, it can be built around basic elective courses (undergraduate or graduate), which exist at some universities. Few of these programs are offered today, but they can be found. However, the programs vary widely, and care should be taken to ensure that the focus of the selected program is on how to operate the business in a world of integrated IT applications and not only on additional technical training. Technical training is important, but the education discussed here is about business management. The development of more of these educational programs is crucial to the ultimate goal of developing a workforce that has the understanding of how to deploy and manage an ERP environment to produce the potential business benefits. This doesn't stop at go-live; it is a career-long journey to achieve the true potential of one's business. The concept of the Learning Organization started long ago and was clearly defined by Peter Senge in the early 1990s.

 ## SUMMARY

Change is a key component of any ERP implementation work that is done, if it is to achieve the Return on Investment that may be desired and, most certainly, is possible. Change is often viewed as changing "those people," meaning workers in the business whose work methods, style, assignments, and skills are going to be affected by the changes. This, however, avoids recognition of the need for a comprehensive governance program to include oversight of the changes necessary at the executive levels of the organization. Paying attention to these needs and addressing them will require working closely with each executive. Thus, necessary changes can be made within the existing political structure, in order to allow the rest of the change process to work smoothly.

Talking about "you don't understand our politics" or viewing all politics as bad fails to recognize the real issue: all organizations are political, regardless of the extent. Each has a unique political culture. The management of change within that structure must be led by and with a "trusted adviser or mechanic," which will ultimately be one of the most important components of a business's success—or failure. It is our belief that more programs fail for these reasons than the few that have failed because the ERP system cannot successfully produce a business process that will achieve the intended business results. It doesn't help when virtually every corner of the industry continues to provide technical answers to management questions, when the approach should be that management defines the needs and the potential improvements for its organization and then selects the technology appropriate to achieve those results. This argument will never be about ignoring the potential of new technology to change the ways we operate to our benefit. Yet it is about the order of the analysis of business needs and the opportunity to drive technology deployment.

The argument presented here is strictly from a business management and leadership perspective. There are technical details involved, and the ERP applications industry continues to pump out more and sexier technology every year. The problem, however, is to find consultants who know how business operates, understand the political processes that are a necessary part of any organization of humans, recognize the need to adhere religiously to structural tools such as scope documents and critical paths, and have the personal skills to work within the cultural and political environment of an enterprise to ensure that decisions are made as wisely as possible so that the critical path is maintained and the Return on Investment is both expected and realized. This is not a technical process; it is a very human one.

CHAPTER TWELVE

12

Conclusions and Opportunities

"You know the greatest danger facing us is ourselves, an irrational fear of the unknown. But
there's no such thing as the unknown—only things
temporarily hidden, temporarily not understood."

—Captain James Kirk, taken from "Five Leadership
Lessons from James T. Kirk," Forbes

 ## THE JOURNEY

We have come a long way in a relatively short period of time. In business
history, most major changes in the way we analyze business challenges have
taken decades to evolve and gain acceptance. Views on how to understand
and manage workforces—from Frederick Taylor's theories of scientific management as mass production techniques were being created to the social
theories of Lewin, McGregor, Emory, Trist, and others—took nearly a century
to evolve. The beginning of using IT to collect, store, gain access to, and use
data about organizational components and the cross-functional relationships

among them (logical relationships) started in the 1950s but didn't really accelerate until computer technology became widely available to individual workers less than three decades ago.

Anyone older than 40 today has had to relearn much of what we grew up knowing or supposing about the world around us. Instead of journals and workbooks, we now have the Internet, blogs about nearly everything, desktop office systems, social and professional networking sites, mobile devices, and now we are moving to cloud computing and even more mobile applications. These advances in processes and products have caused us to think differently about the world around us and to change the paradigms (cognitive principles) that we use to organize our thinking.

Today, documents can be created on our computers and saved onto a cloud program that will automatically synchronize them with copies of the same files on our other mobile devices, such as iPhones and iPads. Now, we can work on the same document anywhere, anytime, and carry only a small tablet computer with us or perhaps not even that. The point of this is that it has caused us to have to change the way we think about the world we live in. We have learned new tasks, new concepts of how to store, collate, and use information about the world around us. We have also learned to think differently about how all of this fits together and relates to our daily lives, essentially to change the paradigms that we use to organize our thoughts and perceptions. The net result is that our minds have expanded to encompass more and different ways to look at and understand the business world we live in. It is not only about learning new tools, but about learning new concepts and how to organize our thoughts differently. It is said that the brilliance of Einstein or Jobs was not that they were smarter than others whom they worked or competed with, but that they were able to look at the problems they were working on differently (cognitively).

The world of integrated business applications has also experienced the same explosion of technology, as developers have figured out how to use modern tools and the exponentially expanding speed of systems, to integrate the logic of how business functions, from logistics and financial recording to human relations, into one comprehensive system. In doing so, they have exposed logical relationships between functions and processes that have always existed but were either too obscure to see or too complex to be analyzed and managed. Using this new knowledge to analyze and organize these functions has been the greatest challenge to business leaders in the last two decades. During that time, software vendors have developed functionality from simple functions such as goods movements and financial recording to more complex functions such as customer relationships and supply chain management.

In addition, vendors have learned the logical effects of actions taken in each function and have created fully integrated software to transact, collect, collate, and report on these transactions. Along with this, we have created a rapidly expanding set of tools to deal with complexity, from project management concepts and training and business process management programs to organizational development and organizational change management, helping us effectively evolve using all of these technological advancements to improve business performance.

 ## THE NEXT STEP

What we have presented in this book takes another look at the role of integrated ERP systems in the enterprise. Our recommendation is that just as we have learned a different way of viewing and using the personal technology tools, we also need to take a different view of integrated systems and how they relate to developing a vision for our businesses and establish a new paradigm for how to use them. The new knowledge of logical relationships that has resulted from designing, implementing, and operating these systems has provided us with this opportunity. Essentially, we conclude that the following five cognitive shifts are required:

1. **Return on Investment** should be viewed as an undiscovered asset of the corporation that should be pursued and recovered. This view of potential returns turns the view around from developing projects and then looking for potential benefits to cataloguing the benefits that are logically possible. This view also helps the business organize a strategic approach to managing ERP work to achieve the benefits over time. A corollary that results from this cognitive shift is that ERP projects should produce tangible benefits that are well defined, are fully supported by management, and have the expectation that the results will be achieved.

2. **Business process management** should be viewed as being package enabled. This means that business process designs are created through rigorous investigation of current state problems and a detailed analysis of logical relationships. Thus, the proposed process designs should always be designed within the logic of the ERP systems. The only exceptions should be when cost benefit analyses between ERP-supported processes and

proprietary designs demonstrate a clear financial benefit for the proprietary design. When this is the case, the proprietary design should be "integrated" into the existing ERP backbone.

3. **Business culture, politics, and organization** should be viewed as a natural part of any enterprise and the emphasis placed on learning how to use business culture, politics, and organization to support the transformation program and deliver the planned Return on Investment. If there are organizational development programs that the business decides to engage in, they need to be complimentary to and not competitive with the ongoing stream of Return on Investment–based ERP programs. Although ERP conversions may well point out weaknesses in these attributes of organizations and spur leadership to change them, the ERP program cannot become embroiled in the politics of these issues and must continue to use the existing framework to achieve results.

4. **IT strategy** should be viewed as a continuous series of smaller (not necessarily small but sized for success measured by Return on Investment) projects conducted sequentially or perhaps overlapping at times. The intent of this applications strategy is to rationalize all proposed and backlogged ERP work, organize it into logical groupings, and establish Return on Investment–based justifications on each, while organizing the governance process around delivering intended results.

5. **Workforce readiness** should be viewed from the perspective of a Learning Organization, where the collective knowledge and skills of the workforce at all levels are viewed as a key to creating a more effective and successful enterprise. Programs should be put in place to support education at all levels and in every competency that is used within the business so that the collective ability is enhanced in support of the overall ERP programs. Continuing education can no longer be considered a nice academic idea but must become part of everyday business leadership.

Based on new awareness and perspectives in these five business components, the following should be the guiding principles for the overall program:

1. **Program governance** should be established, to oversee both the individual and the collective project stream as day-to-day oversight of the project teams. Also, this function must serve as coach, counselor, and facilitator at the executive level to help resolve problems that affect issues not within the resolving ability of the project teams.

2. **Organizational change management** programs must be expanded beyond just the skills transitions, communications, and training programs with the current workforce and must be merged with the program governance function such that organizational development and organizational change management issues caused by the ERP transformation can be resolved at both the worker and the executive levels simultaneously.

 ## LEADERSHIP

Finally, all of these new realizations of how the organization works at a business logic level, along with how changes can achieve business benefits, must be incorporated into an expanded view of leadership's role in ensuring that knowledge exists within the organization to make effective use of this opportunity. Vision, alignment, motivation, and inspiration remain the hallmarks of how leadership differs from management. Yet this vision must include an evaluation of collective leadership knowledge of how business processes operate, as well as a program to either fill the holes or determine how to support executives during this period.

Although some organizations have evolved during the last couple of decades and currently incorporate some of these principles in their leadership and management approach, we have found that most others have not and remain constrained by organizational paradigms (cognitive principles) that may have served them well years ago but now serve to limit their corporate effectiveness. As leaders consider the concepts presented in this book, they should take stock of the insights and figure out how to incorporate them into programs where they find understanding lacking. What action is needed and figuring out how to incorporate these insights will vary from business to business, but the combination of the new insights, in some form, provides the opportunity for any business to improve its organizational performance using ERP systems and to achieve the Return on Investment that is available and ready to be recovered.[1] The next discussion provides a stepwise approach to evaluate these principles in any business and provides an opportunity to analyze and incorporate those concepts or programs that will enhance organizational effectiveness. As much as this is a formula for success, it must be used to tailor an approach that is appropriate for any individual business.

THE PATH FORWARD

To recap the path offered in this book, the following seven steps need to be taken or retaken, in order to get an organization ready to achieve the business benefits that are possible and available and to deal with redesign issues that will inevitably occur at all levels of the enterprise:

1. Create a vision.
2. Foster leadership education.
3. Catalogue Return on Investment potential.
4. Create an analysis for each of the five streams.
5. Merge the analyses.
6. Establish program governance.
7. Establish executive support function.

This action plan for implementation describes a change in the management approach and in the operations, rather than a onetime project to achieve a onetime result. Here is a detailed breakdown of the seven steps.

1. **Create a vision.** Establish a vision for the corporation that includes a broad view of the objectives that will be included. We tend to think of corporate vision at the CEO levels as being focused on products, markets, and strategic goals. Optimization of the business processes toward the objective of finding the lowest cost and the highest quality, business processes must be a part of that vision. Regardless of the business involved, inefficiencies in how the business operates are best represented by any undiscovered or unrecovered potential Return on Investment that creates an opportunity for competitors to gain an advantage in the market. The best defense against competition is to achieve industry-leading efficiency.

2. **Foster leadership education.** Conduct education for the leadership team (perhaps at several levels but surely at the executive suite) on the impact and process of evaluating opportunities. As discussed, we are dealing with a transformational change in the way we understand and manage our business. It is unlikely, with all of the cultural and political roadblocks that have grown over the years, that this will suddenly become intuitive. It may be impossible to simply build on what exists, incrementally, without continuing to suffer from the Law of Unintended

Consequences. In Michael Hammer and James Champy's approach from *Re-Engineering the Corporation*, this is the difference between incremental and transformational change.[2]

3. **Catalogue Return on Investment Potential.** Create a process to define Return on Investment for each investment project during the life of the program. Remember that this is a shared opportunity and although a business will never achieve a perfect business process where no more improvement is possible, the goal is always in that direction. It will change as the fundamental nature of the business also changes with the introduction of new products, new markets, new competition, and perhaps new company structures through acquisition or divestiture of businesses.

4. **Create an analysis for each of the five streams.** Define and analyze approaches to each of the following aspects, based on a new paradigm:
   - Return on Investment opportunity identification
   - Business process management
   - Cultural/political assessment
   - IT strategy
   - Workforce readiness

5. **Merge the analyses.** Bring the five streams together and analyze the interactions among them. For example, if the business process design approach calls for each department to evaluate its own needs and decide how to address its issues from a cultural/political perspective, then using a cross-functional business process design approach will simply result in frustration at all levels. If education and training of the workforce are going to be spread over many years for budgetary purposes, the ability to get business process changes implemented in the short term may be severely affected.

6. **Establish program governance.** Develop a standing governance process that addresses the four elements of governance that are needed—an Executive Steering Committee, a Program Governance Office with day-to-day coordination and integration of the design, implementation and organizational change management processes, and a fully staffed project management function.

7. **Establish an executive support function.** Specifically design a "trusted adviser" role in support of executive leadership that identifies issues as they arise and can broker design decisions based on a full realization of the potential impact of different decisions or even of no decisions. Often

organizations may believe that they are mature enough in their leadership to resolve political issues in staff meetings; however, we have found that rarely to be the case. The use of a trusted adviser who is non-threatening and focused on the economic good for the company can improve this ability.

Because this is intended to be a continuous improvement process, it is also time to manage all of the other improvement processes, not necessarily as part of this program, but within the same framework. The inclusion of these other areas is intended to

- Ensure that precious resources are properly allocated between projects.
- Guarantee that changes derived from one process are not at odds with changes from another one to make sure that Return on Investment is not a competition but is delivered through the coordinated management of these processes.
- Guard against a return to the "program du jour" tendency that is prevalent in many organizations.

We have tended to look at ERP systems as just more IT technology that has to be used to operate a business. The approach presented in this book is that while this statement is true, it doesn't go far enough to demonstrate the real opportunity that IT technology presents. It does not lead to understanding the current challenges and how this technology can be used to produce business results. We are in the middle of the most dramatic, exciting, and, yes, challenging revelations in how components of businesses operate at the detail level. Although there will always be yet another set of unintended consequences, we are really on the brink of our ability to eliminate many of the archaic aspects of business processes that have been created in the functional world. This will require us to move our thinking and leadership firmly and diligently into the postfunctional business world. In turn, this calls for a new view of leadership and change in the integrated business world.

 ## THE LAW OF UNINTENDED CONSEQUENCES

Let's return to the Law of Unintended Consequences one more time. The functional world has always been integrated, where virtually every action in one function has consequences in all of the others, some dramatic, some minimal, but always having consequences. Over the years, management theories have identified and quantified these relationships and impacts, but as businesses have grown larger and more complex, the ability to conceptualize all intended and unintended results of actions has become more and more difficult.

Now, with the advent of ERP software systems, the process of identifying connection points and understanding how both positive and negative consequences not only are created but can also be predicted has brought the challenge from out of the dark into the full light of day. Along with this revelation comes a whole set of new challenges for leaders and process owners.

Let's look at one more dramatic example of this principle. During the 1960s and the 1970s, the fatality rate for open-wheel racers had risen due to increased speeds and handling, to the point where more and more deaths occurred each year. As a result, steps were taken to make the sport safer, and one of the directions it took was to use the concept of dissipating energy in a crash so that the driver didn't absorb the entire force during an accident. Consequently, the monocoque chassis was developed, along with external parts of the vehicle that would dissemble, taking a lot of the energy away from the driver in a crash. Also, the guardrails were moved up to the edge of the racing surface such that a vehicle that was out of control would be channeled in a straight line. All of this resulted in the fatality rate falling over a number of years; however, as good as these effects seem from this story, there were unintended consequences.

In some cases, as the external parts of vehicles separated from the car at high speeds, they traveled farther and sometimes even flew into the spectator areas, causing injuries and fatalities. In addition, while driver fatalities were decreasing, the immediate presence of hard surfaces (guardrails) was creating more injuries, and the added confidence of drivers meant a more daring style of racing. All of these unintended consequences were not foreseen by the additional benefits of the changes. In response to vehicle parts flying into stands, high retaining fences were constructed, as well as safer barriers (energy-absorbing guardrails) added to the tracks.

Again, this reduced injuries and fatalities to the point where they are uncommon today; however, as recent events have pointed out, these advances have also created unintended consequences. Barriers and fences built to absorb impact and catch parts separated from the vehicles, along with again increased speeds and risk taking, have led to another fatality. Far from being an indictment of this sport or the occasional unfortunate events such as this, our point is that it is very clear that every action taken to improve safety has done so (the numbers are unimpeachable), but there have also been unintended consequences that will once again need to be analyzed and dealt with.

So, how does this apply to business systems, where the only fatalities that generally occur due to unintended consequences are careers, rather than lives? This analogy is actually a pretty close one, and we have only to look at the second example cited in Chapter 1. Every action taken over years, from opening distribution centers that ordered directly from manufacturing to adding cutters to increasing safety stock, ended up having consequences that were not foreseen and ultimately nearly destroyed the company.

Another example from the same business may also help explain this. Printing plates must be free of surface defects, which will end up "printing," perhaps in the middle of glossy pictures, thereby ruining the picture. Consequently, as the plates are produced, they either go through an automated machine inspection process or are hand-inspected by workers. Occasionally, defective plates may be experienced in a customer shop that had failed to be detected by inspection. Typically, the next order from the distribution center would specify that the order had to be "double-inspected," which meant that two workers had to inspect the material in sequence. There is a well-known psychological principle that this will cause each worker to look less carefully because they both know that there will be another inspection, with the net result that small defects are even less likely to be detected. Thus, the net effect is that quality decreases. One can guess that the next order required "triple inspection," again with further unintended consequences.

How does this apply to the subject of this book? While improvement programs have focused on business improvements, many have met with either failure or, if successful, with less than anticipated results. This is not because of myopic studies or ill-advised functional programs to produce positive benefits, but it is because the interrelationships between business components are logical and have always existed and oftentimes were not understood. The challenge is to recognize that the type of opportunities presented by the implementation and operation of ERP platforms is not the result of things changing in business but is the result of ERP programs exposing these relationships and issues that have been created over the years in a purely functional environment. Far from being unexpected or traumatic, these changes represent more knowledge of the relationship between the pieces, just as James Orlicky defined the relationship between parts, assemblies, and bills of materials more than 50 years ago.[3]

From a business perspective, it is almost like the current discoveries in physics on the expansion of the universe or the limits of the speed of light. Just as these discoveries, if proven valid, will cause rethinking of all of the aspects of Einstein's theory, so it is also true for the opportunities presented by ERP systems. If properly implemented and used, ERP systems will cause a redefinition of the relationship between all of the components of the business. To believe that this would not call for dramatically different cognitive and governance approaches, one would simply be failing to recognize the potential of this time in our history.

Now, let's pause and reflect on the program described here. It would be easy to think of this as the next program du jour or the next best idea. One aspect of the governance program recommended here is that these competing programs must all come under the general auspices of the Program Governance Office. This recommendation is not so much to control the programs but to ensure that they are not in competition or opposition to the others. All newly recommended programs must be evaluated by this function so that knowledge of the five analyses and the merging of these evaluations remain evergreen, or current—what engineers refer to as "as-built."

Some years ago, a large company dispatched organizational change management practitioners to conduct group surveys or interviews on the workforce's perception of change in the organization. They started with the question of whether the audience felt that there had been too much or too little change in the previous couple of years. The best answer was that there had actually been too little real change and too much creation of the perception of change in the organization. That would explain why, although the audience felt as if there had been a lot of change, people could not define exactly what of value had actually changed or what Return on Investment had been achieved during that time. As a follow-up example, another company went through a period of time where the change driver was the process of centralizing or decentralizing the business, which in large corporations can be extraordinarily disruptive. In a conversation with the CEO, he expressed his view that if his company was centralized in core functions, he would seek to decentralize it; however, if it were decentralized, he would seek to centralize it. His view was that neither organizational concept was "correct" and that the real value in any programs such as this lies in how one delivers results— whether by customer satisfaction, cost reduction, or other measures. As Andrew Spanyi points out in his book *Operational Leadership*: "The principal skills most frequently lacking in managers are the means for developing a view of the business in terms of the cross-functional activities that constitute the company's value chain and the means for creating value for customers."[4]

Ultimately, change programs that do not focus on creating customer value are not properly tied to delivering business results. The need to create a change engine to allow for traditional processes to be redesigned and implemented has been known for years as organizations have grown. The problem with this approach, however, is that unless this change process includes developing new information about how the components relate to one another and provides a process to deal with the intransigence of previous designs, the likelihood of positive and permanent change is very low.

What may be different from previous times is that the transition to modern ERP business applications is not generally an option that has been selected for the purposes of driving change where there is at least a visible target in mind. It is, instead, driven by the revolution in technology that has allowed these systems to be developed and delivered effectively and economically to support business processes. Many business groups we have worked with either see this as a purely technological solution to problems that they don't think they have or they see themselves as victims. Neither of these views is productive and certainly neither of them allows for a solution to the problem or a long-term commitment to continuous improvement.

This does, however, come with a host of new issues and challenges to the enterprise and the attendant skill sets required to define, design, implement, optimize, and operate. Using these ERP systems produces significantly more challenges to the existing leadership teams in today's corporations. We can no longer afford to pretend that the exercise is academic. New competitors will use the early phases of their business to analyze these relationships defined in ERP terms and will implement programs and systems that will allow them to leapfrog older, more developed companies. This business process technology is absolutely subject to the same laws that manufacturing technologies have been over the years.

The same issues apply, incidentally, to university business schools. In a majority of schools, the faculty have grown and developed in the same functional/technical environment as today's business leaders. Consequently, collegiate-level business education will also be challenged to develop a fully integrated approach to teaching business disciplines. It is this symbiotic relationship between education and business that requires future business education programs to truly integrate the disciplines of accounting, finance, management, marketing, logistics, information systems, and so on. To remain in the past, where each business discipline was taught without reference to the other business disciplines, created a silo learning experience for the business student; in other words, the student studied manufacturing but did not study manufacturing's relationship to procurement, distribution, logistics, sales, distribution, and so on. Hopefully, collegiate business education programs will soon begin to aggressively change their approach to the study of business disciplines by requiring their students to study the integrative capabilities of each business discipline's relationship with other business disciplines within each business program of study.

 ## HOW INSIGHT RELATES TO MANUFACTURING

Some years back, a business team was commissioned to acquire a new technology, design a U.S. plant, and build it to manufacture a new product. In developing the business case, it was determined that in economic terms, this was going to be an attractive product line, from a performance and margin basis. Even a fledgling economist knows that high margins and lack of competition create a business opportunity for others who will, in addition to building their own capacity, also reduce the cost of manufacturing through continued research and develop into new types of equipment and technology. The business case said—build the plant, sell it out at $x/lb margin, and expand it in the first five years, during which it would continue to make outstanding margins. Then, however, the company should either sell the plant or decommission it because new manufacturing techniques would have rendered it noncompetitive from a cost-of-manufacturing standpoint.

So far, this is a great story and, in fact, was one that resulted in outstanding success. Financially, the targets were met; competitors did exactly what had been predicted; and it resulted in the anticipated downward pressure on prices. Eventually, the company abandoned the business plan and, in the ensuing years, lost everything that it had gained and more. The point here is that the same is happening today as new companies enter markets, without all of the old company baggage in business processes and IT applications. Only a new focus on understanding how ERP applications and new approaches to maintain competitive cost structures can prevent the natural decline in productivity and profitability.

 ## THE STORY IS ECONOMIC

The key in this process, as in the story in Chapter 2 of the CIO who led by limiting the cost of IT applications, has to be an economic one. If there are really no tangible business benefits from doing something, what in the world would be the argument for doing it? Whether this involves cost reduction, manufacturing efficiencies, improved market conditions (either offensively or defensively), or something completely different, there is always a way to define the financial incentives to invest in any program of this type. If business leaders give themselves a pass on this because of cultural/political issues, they will always subvert the process of change that is necessary to achieve results. So, if this is true, we need a better way to manage the continuous improvement process that incorporates not only all of the disciplines involved but also provides a means to work through organizational issues that are raised at the highest levels of the enterprise. That is the model presented here.

More than three decades ago, Phil Crosby, in his book *Quality Is Free*, listed his 14 steps to a quality program, with the fourteenth step being "Do It All Over Again."[5] Dr. W. Edwards Deming, in *Out of the Crisis*, in his 14 steps, concluded with "Establish a Continuous Improvement Program."[6] The additional value in Dr. Deming's approach is that it turned the introduction of quality programs into a process, rather than a series of events. As the quality programs of the 1980s have evolved through Six Sigma, lean manufacturing, Lean Six Sigma, and many others, they have always worked to maintain a permanent quality to improving business processes. Why this didn't carry over into the influx of these powerful ERP applications platforms is likely the result of several effects:

- Y2K issues that made conversion from legacy applications containing the year numbering conflicts a high priority.
- Lack of real knowledge of the relationship between ERP platforms and business performance that is different from more traditional approaches.
- Programmatic, rather than process-focused, views of improvement programs.

All of these streams must now be incorporated into a single improvement process stream that will survive the completion of any one project and become a permanent part of business cultures. Because this is really a control and predictability issue, the starting point for much of this may come from the CFO function or, more broadly, from the enterprise risk management responsibility of the board of directors.

 SUMMARY

There will always be a need to tailor approaches to any individual company or any group of leaders. What we have presented throughout this book is what we believe to be universal truths about necessary changes in leadership styles and techniques to allow companies to keep up with exploding technological changes, while maintaining competitiveness in their marketplaces. The bottom line in all of this is really simple, though: It is always about the business. While tricks and shortcuts will continue to be advocated by some, to achieve these ends, and while software vendors will continue to sell new functionality that can supposedly, by itself, resolve these issues, the answer will always be hard work. The improvements in technology tools enable and institutionalize changes to business processes that have the potential to produce tangible benefits. The work of changing business processes to maximize Return on Investment using ERP applications—just as the book's title says—will always be the hard work of leading organizations in the integrated business world.

 NOTES

1. Marvin R. Weisbord, *Productive Workplaces: Dignity, Meaning, and Community in the 21st Century* (San Francisco: Jossey-Bass Inc., 1987); John Kotter, *A Force for Change: How Leadership Differs from Management* (New York: Free Press, 1990).
2. Michael Hammer and James Champy, *Re-engineering the Corporation: A Manifesto for Business Revolution* (New York: Harper Business Essentials, 1993).
3. James Orlicky, *Material Requirements Planning* (New York: McGraw-Hill, 1975).
4. Andrew Spanyi, *Operational Leadership* (New York: Business Expert Press, 2010).
5. Philip B. Crosby, *Quality Is Free: The Art of Making Quality Certain* (New York: McGraw-Hill, 1979).
6. W. Edwards Deming, *Out of the Crisis* (Cambridge: Massachusetts Institute of Technology, Center for Advanced Engineering Study, 1982, 1986).

Postscript

This book has focused extensively on issues that concern capturing Returns on Investment using ERP applications as they are generally available or used today. Our intent has been to establish that

1. There is much work left to be done simply by resolving issues with applications that are already installed but are not delivering the intended business results; resolving these issues can produce the business benefits that were originally envisioned.
2. There is an unrealized opportunity for companies with core ERP applications installed to capitalize on Return on Investment—based programs to deploy shelf-ware (components of ERP that are owned but not yet installed) to achieve benefits.
3. The current ERP work that is called for also includes resolving issues that have been created through acquisitions or divestitures, either to adopt common processes or to decide strategically how to "integrate" them. This is to provide a single view of corporate performance, one version of the truth. It acknowledges that there may be utility in keeping current systems in place, despite the fact that they may be constructed quite differently, and deal with standardizing results with business intelligence toolsets. Remember that this has to include the assumption that the applications suite installed in each business is able to provide optimized business results for that business. If one or more of them are not, then developing a strategic approach to resolving this issue should be awarded a high priority.

If it is the case that optimization work is well advanced or if organizational strategy is focused on achieving this state on a believable timeline, it is also worth taking a look at where continuing Return on Investment—based projects may come from in the future. The fact of the matter is that for most businesses, the previously mentioned three points should keep them busy implementing or refining their applications for years to come, all the while realizing significant tangible benefits. While they are achieving that goal, regardless of the timeline, the process put in place should serve to instill

- The expectation of success for IT projects to perform as planned.
- The concept that all ERP investments should be based on Return on Investment, perhaps with rare exceptions.
- The adoption of a leadership and change model that is appropriate for managing in an integrated business world will have been institutionalized in the organization.

With this in mind, it is a good time to also take a look at what the future might hold. This is important so that the organization can be better prepared to deal with the constant hype in the media and from colleagues about new and glitzy technology. Earlier in this book, we mentioned a transformation program two decades ago that had been based on rewriting legacy applications (all that we had at that time) to redesign business processes to help save a business that was in serious financial difficulty. We mentioned that at the successful end of the initial turnaround plan, the work group produced an IT strategy that would continue to use new technology to produce improved business results and that the business decided to revert to the philosophy that IT investments were a cost to be avoided whenever possible. With whatever success a business is able to achieve with the program described in this book, a point will inevitably be reached where there will be advocates for "enough is enough." That is the point where staff groups may be tempted to revert to again seeing themselves as the hapless victims, with an image of themselves as a high-performing executive group that is unable to manage the ever-increasing explosion of technology. In our opinion, this is more of a political process than a real one and is a situation that should be avoided whenever possible. Evaluating future technology, at least for awareness, is always a good approach, particularly since the business has just undertaken an extensive look at what IT applications can accomplish. This is a good time to relate potential future developments to real-time business improvements.

First, the odds that a business has achieved perfect performance based on any design of its business process are unlikely. Second, every business is connected to some outside business world, which most certainly has not suddenly become stable. In fact, most of the business literature deals with the acceleration of change throughout the business world. There will continue to be new markets, new customers, new vendors, new acquisitions, new products, new leaders, and many more factors that the applications platform every business operates on must be able to handle. The ability to avoid complacency will always be a challenge for any business, and once the momentum of change is successfully established and proved, every effort should be made to maintain that momentum.

Following are several areas of interest that the Program Governance Office, working as the operational arm of the ESC, should continue to explore for new opportunities:

1. **Customers.** Any business is only as good as how close it is to understanding and meeting its customers' needs. Development continues to enrich functionality of CRM systems, both with improved visibility into tools to manage markets and customers and with the ability to automate some of the customer-facing processes. This applies both for sales and for tailoring products to meet specific customers' needs.

2. **Vendors.** As well as the work done to improve internal systems and controls, vendors, in most cases, have been working to improve their internal systems and functionality. The improvement in your vendors' control and delivery systems can offer opportunities to connect your applications to theirs more closely. These opportunities can be as diverse as automating some aspects of the supply chain to creating vendor certification programs based on statistical evaluations and many more.

3. **Products.** New or improved products are necessary to remain in a competitive position in virtually any industry. Better capabilities to tie together research and development functions with vendors or partners, who can participate in these activities, provide an opportunity to shorten development cycles to get "first to market." Particularly in a world where various functions may be outsourced and yet remain fully integrated into the primary business systems, new functionality can provide better control and more predictability. A good example of this is in the fashion industry, where designs may be done in-house and then prototypes built by contractors, factories producing the articles under contract, and perhaps logistics outsourcing the systems.

4. **Automation.** As you improve management of the entire supply chain, greater functionality and speed will provide the opportunity to create better visibility, as well as automation up and down your supply chain.

The real value is the ability to see further in either direction, as improved forecasting, reduced inventory of all partners, improved manufacturing efficiencies based on optimized product development, or many other areas can now be managed more proactively. It is important to note that just as it is possible to view inefficiencies in your business for improvement, it is more and more possible to view these same issues throughout a multi-tiered supply chain. Inventory and inefficiency anywhere in the supply chain amount to a cost, and that cost must be borne by someone up or down the chain. Helping your vendor improve inventory levels and on-time performance through more accurate forecasting, for example, can lower costs for your vendor and provide an opportunity for you to share in lower prices.

5. **Human resources.** Managing human capital, from recruiting to work-force education, while training workers in improved work methods throughout the entire business cycle, offers enhanced opportunities to optimize productivity and accuracy in all functions. Today, recruiting is depending more and more heavily on social media, which has to be merged into the entire acquisition process. Also, employee development and organizational control issues can be managed using ERP applications when the business case makes sense.

6. **Data.** That's really data, data, and data. Every transaction you create in the system produces more data. Some of this data is innocuous, at least as it is used today. Other data is crucial for various reporting needs, some is key for analysis and audit, and yet more is important for understanding markets and other external actors. You have only to look at Walmart to see how data can be used to derive business benefits. In its well-publicized case, learning how to analyze massive amounts of consumer transac-tional data was one of the competencies that allowed it to become the largest retailer in the world. The real power of data, however, as discussed earlier in the book, is to open up the thought process to discover infor-mation and undertake an analysis to provide paths for businesses to gain a competitive advantage. Although this is expressed in today's analytical capabilities as providing business content and presentation layers, it can also open up thinking into what additional data we might collect at the transaction or master data level that could then be used for even more effective market analysis. We have really just begun to identify all of the ways this area can be mined for valuable insights. Beyond the simple use of existing data is the opportunity to develop ways to make the data

smarter at the point of capture. This can be done at times by expanding transactions to include identification, capture means, and improved accuracy of what is entered into and gathered by each transaction.

7. **Speed.** Earlier, we mentioned that incorrect information supplied faster is simply faster, not better. This, however, is not meant to imply that faster cannot create a competitive advantage. As data systems become more capable of providing an accurate analysis more quickly and more nimbly, the ability to move business knowledge closer to the point that it is used also becomes more powerful. This is the promise of technology such as in-memory computing, cloud, and mobility, which offer such promise as long as the fundamentals have been implemented correctly. Over time, speeds will continue to increase, business content at analytical levels will become more powerful, and we will get to the point where data will become a component at the point of sale.

8. **More effective management oversight.** With the advent of enterprise risk management programs, some of the identification, transaction, collection, collation, analysis, and reporting capabilities of ERP applications will provide more opportunities. We will be able to improve our ability to use reporting systems to create cross-checks in large complex systems to ensure that businesses are operating consistently with what is being reported. This ability to be creative in how these "risk management" reports are visualized and delivered has the potential not only to ensure the accuracy of reporting but to improve the stability and the sustainability of our businesses as well.

 SUMMARY

The point here is that these future benefits are all dependent on achieving optimization of the use of current applications. This will be completed by actually recovering the Return on Investment that was initially envisioned for the programs and that, to a great degree, still exists as an unrealized asset of the corporation. Once we have completed the basic homework and recovered what we left behind, the ability to lead our businesses to competitive advantage in an integrated business world doesn't stop; it just continues to provide tangible business benefits for as far as we can see. Change is the paradigm that we are learning to accept as the single constant in the business ecosystem we operate, and speed is the driving characteristic of that change.

If change is constant, speed is accelerating, and thus competition will only become more challenging. Maximizing the Return on Investment in our use of ERP applications is rapidly becoming a critical success factor in deciding which businesses will flourish and which ones will ultimately fail.

Although the tools may be the technology, and the skills to implement may be technical, the leadership required to lead tomorrow's successful enterprise is a contextual awareness of how ERP applications can be used to produce tangible business benefits.

That awareness has emerged during the last two decades and will define business success for as far as we can see. We, the authors, hope that the concepts you have learned in this book will provide the necessary perspectives to create the competitive advantage you need for your future success.

About the Authors

Arthur J. Worster is currently the director of Corporate Applicability at the College of Business Administration at Central Michigan University. In addition, he is an adjunct faculty member in the online M.B.A. program, working with the courses in the ERP Concentration and the ERP Graduate Certificate, using SAP. Mr. Worster also provides consulting services through Worster Associates, LLC, to clients on ERP Program Governance and Workforce Educational programs to improve the ability of companies to achieve expected benefits from their ERP investments.

Mr. Worster has experience in executive leadership positions in the chemical and services industries, as well as with graduate business school programs, for more than 40 years. He is a graduate of the State University of New York at Buffalo with a B.A. degree in philosophy and economics. He spent a year at Buffalo in Economics Graduate School studying developing economies until entering the U.S. Air Force as an officer. After nearly five years of commanding aircraft maintenance training schools, Mr. Worster left the U.S. Air Force and entered industry. He held progressive positions in manufacturing operations, from first line supervisor to division operations director, during the ensuing 13 years, which included overseeing the design, construction, and commissioning of two major chemical plants. After spending four years leading environment, health, and safety efforts, Mr. Worster became shared services director for a business turnaround, where he became involved in redesigning business processes and overseeing the rewriting of legacy business applications that led to a successful conclusion. He then extended that knowledge, undertaking business process reengineering for an additional 13 specialty chemical divisions. During this time, he led a selection process that concluded with the selection of SAP as the business transformation toolset to be implemented across the business group. In 1996, the business group Mr. Worster supported was being divested, and Mr. Worster transitioned to the IT services industry to work with clients on business transformation using SAP. After working as director of operations for a boutique SAP consulting company (SLI, Inc.) for nearly two years, Mr. Worster accepted a leadership position with EDS, a large global IT outsourcing company, to work with clients to achieve business benefits from their SAP programs. During the subsequent nine years, Mr. Worster worked directly with clients in program advisory and program leadership roles, including as overall program manager for a large, fixed-price and full-suite, joint-venture SAP business transformation project, where many of the concepts in this book were developed and tested successfully. At the conclusion of this project, Mr. Worster accepted an opportunity to create a global ERP practice for EDS by gathering existing pieces, acquiring companies, and instituting aggressive hiring programs. During a two-year period, Mr. Worster increased the collected size of the consulting organization from approximately 150 to nearly 4,000 globally. He served as global ERP director and chairman of GEMS, Pvt., Ltd., until his retirement from EDS in September 2007. Mr. Worster has now been director of Corporate Applicability, reporting to the dean of Central Michigan University's College of Business Administration, for three years. His work at the university has concentrated on bringing business focus and content to the technical courses taught as part of the Graduate Certificate and M.B.A. programs. Mr. Worster is a contributing author to the *Wiley Journal of Corporate Accounting and Finance*, writing about organizational change management using ERP applications, and has spoken to a number of SAP-related conferences, including SAPPHIRE, State Chapter ASUG meetings, and corporate groups, and has presented Webinars based on his ERP experience.

■ ■ ■

Thomas R. Weirich, Ph.D., CPA, is currently the Jerry & Felicia Campbell Endowed Professor of Accounting at Central Michigan University. He received his B.S. and M.B.A. degrees from Northern Illinois University and a doctorate in accountancy from the University of Missouri-Columbia. Dr. Weirich, the former chair of the School of Accounting, has served on special assignment as the Academic Accounting Fellow to the Office of the Chief Accountant at the U.S. Securities and Exchange Commission in Washington, D.C. He has completed a Faculty in Residence position with a major accounting firm in its Business Fraud & Investigative Services Division, whereby he participated in various fraud and background investigations. He has served as a member of the Technical Working Group for Education in Fraud and Forensic Accounting, funded by the U.S.

Department of Justice, that created the "Model Curriculum in Forensic Accounting." He also served as a consultant to the Public Oversight Board's Panel on Audit Effectiveness. He has recently participated in the SAP Terp-10 Program. Dr. Weirich was recently reappointed by the governor of the State of Michigan to serve on the Michigan State Board of Accountancy. He currently is the chair of the board.

Dr. Weirich has public accounting experience with an international firm, as well as with a local firm. He has served on the Editorial Advisory Board to the *Journal of Accountancy*, as well as being a committee member on the American Accounting Association's Education Committee and the SEC Liaison Committee. He also served on the AICPA's Pre-Certification Executive Education Committee and on the Michigan Association of CPAs' CPE Committee, Fraud Task Force, and the Environmental Issues Committee. In addition, he previously served on the AICPA's Technical Standards Subcommittee-Ethics, as well as on the AICPA's Auditing Subcommittee and Content Committee, related to the CPA exam and the SEC's Regulations Committee. Dr. Weirich currently serves on the AICPA Board of Examiners' Auditing Simulations Subcommittee, which aids in the development of audit simulations for the auditing section of the CPA Examination; on the AICPA's Ethics-Independence/Behavioral Subcommittee; and on the National State Boards of Accountancy's (NASBA) Education and Ethics Committees. Professor Weirich has written numerous articles in professional journals and has served as a business consultant to various organizations on related accounting issues. Dr. Weirich has been the recipient of the School of Accounting/Beta Alpha Psi's Outstanding Teacher Award, the Ameritech/ SBC Teaching Award, the College of Business Dean's Teaching Award, the Michigan Association of Governing Boards' Distinguished Faculty Award, and the Michigan Association of CPAs' Distinguished Achievement in Accounting Education Award. He has received the national Beta Alpha Psi "Outstanding Faculty Advisor" Award. He has served as an expert witness for the SEC and on other cases. He has also served as mayor of the City of Mt. Pleasant.

He has developed educational cases that have been accepted and published by the AICPA's Case Development Program and is currently developing SAP/audit—related cases for his auditing courses. Dr. Weirich is the lead coauthor of a popular text titled *Accounting & Auditing Research: Tools and Strategies*, seventh edition, which is used by a number of universities and by CPA firms and corporations for staff training purposes. He also coauthored

Mastering the FASB Codification and eIFRS: A Case Approach. His primary teaching and research areas include auditing, financial accounting, forensic accounting, and SEC issues.

■ ■ ■

Frank J. C. Andera, Ed.D., is currently the director of the SAP University Alliance Program and a professor in the Business Information Systems Department at Central Michigan University (CMU). He received his B.S. from the University of South Dakota, an M.S. from Northern State College, and a doctorate in higher education administration, business cognate, from the University of Montana. Dr. Andera has served as director of the SAP University Alliance Program at CMU since its inception in 1997. CMU is one of the original five universities in North America to join the SAP University Alliance Program. Under his guidance, CMU's graduate and undergraduate programs have become leaders in North America in educating students about one of the world's most sophisticated software products, SAP. Enterprise Resource Planning (ERP) concentrations are a part of the on-campus M.B.A. and M.S.I.S. programs, as well as the online M.B.A. program. ERP concentrations are also available to undergraduate students in the B.S.B.A. degree. CMU's undergraduate and graduate students can choose from more than 16 courses, providing students with the opportunity to complete ERP exercises in their courses using SAP software. More than 9,000 CMU graduate and undergraduate students have gained experience in ERP using the SAP software. Also offered as a B.S.B.A. core course, required of all business students, is a junior-level business course, Integrated Business Experience. In this course, students have the opportunity to experience the integrative capabilities of an ERP system by running a fictitious business using a real-life SAP system. This simulation prepares students to participate in teams using various SAP reports on sales, procurement, manufacturing, distribution, and so on, competing against other teams for as many as four to six quarters, and continuing to make decisions based on their company's performance. This simulation is also used in the M.B.A. and M.S.I.S. graduate-level programs.

Dr. Andera has helped CMU's SAP University Alliance Program become one of the leading university programs in North America in offering TERP10 SAP ERP Integration of Business Processes Certification Academies. This certification is the golden trophy of any SAP University Alliance Program and is a two-week, intensive program of study, culminating with a certification exam.

CMU has offered more than 30 TERP10 SAP ERP Integration of Business Processes Certification Academies since 2000 as a part of its graduate and undergraduate degrees.

Dr. Andera serves as the adviser to CMU's SAP University Alliance Student Group. This professional student group has presented at America's SAP User Group (ASUG) meetings in Michigan, Ohio, Indiana, Minnesota, and Illinois. As adviser to this student group, Dr. Andera has networked and personally met with lead project members who are either actively using or planning to implement ERP solutions using SAP at such notable companies as John Deere, 3M, MillerCoors, Harley-Davidson, Quaker Oats, Dow Chemical, All State, Dow Corning, St. Jude Medical, Steelcase, Compuware, and Blue Cross Blue Shield of Michigan. He and his students were also invited to present at a SAPPHIRE meeting in Los Angeles.

Dr. Andera has served as chairperson of the Business Information Systems Department and has received the Award of Merit for Innovation and Best Practices presented by the Mid-Continent East Association to Advance Collegiate Schools of Business. His submission was titled "Integration of ERP Concepts into a Diverse College of Business Curriculum using SAP Software." He has received the College of Business Deans' Teaching Award at Central Michigan University, and he has written numerous articles in professional journals. Dr. Andera has presented at international meetings of the International Association of Computer Information Systems, SAP Academic Conferences Americas, the Athens Institute for Education and Research, SAPPHIRE, the Hawaii International Conference on Business, the Association to Advance Collegiate Schools of Business, and the American Association of Higher Education.

About the Website

Please visit this book's website at www.wiley.com/go/usingerp to download companion and auxiliary materials useful in evaluating the business fundamentals and their relationships that may be preventing successful achievement of potential Return on Investment.

The materials on the website provide guidelines to designing and executing customized programs appropriate to individual companies for the development of continuous improvement programs.

The materials include:

I. PowerPoint Presentation: "Maximizing Return on Investment Using ERP Applications"
II. Materials for Leadership Evaluation
    a. Outline for One-Day Leadership Evaluation Workshop
    b. Leadership Workshop for an Integrated Business World
    c. References on Leadership
III. Materials for Contextual Evaluation
    a. Return on Investment
    b. Business Process Management
    c. Culture, Politics, and Organization
    d. IT Strategy
    e. Workforce Education
IV. Materials for Consolidation and Program Governance
    a. Consolidating Learning from Contextual Evaluation
    b. Establishing a Continuous Improvement Program Governance Function
    c. Organizational Change Management/Organizational Development
V. Materials for Curriculum Development for Graduate Business Schools
    a. Use as Business Fundamentals for IT Management Concentration
    b. Use as Graduate School Leadership Course

VI. Case Studies

Please feel free to provide feedback about your experiences creating a customized approach to delivering business benefits using ERP applications, or to request help in developing programs, by contacting Art Worster at ajworster@verizon.net.

Index